Stella
25. Feby 1904
H₃

2⅟-

17/6

SAMUEL PEPYS

LOVER OF MUSIQUE

Samuel Pepys

Master of the Corporation

1676 and 1685

Trinity House, London

SAMUEL PEPYS

LOVER OF MUSIQUE

BY

SIR FREDERICK BRIDGE, M.V.O., Mus. Doc.

KING EDWARD PROFESSOR OF MUSIC IN THE UNIVERSITY
OF LONDON ; ORGANIST OF WESTMINSTER ABBEY

" Musique is the thing of the world that I love most."
—DIARY, *July* 30, 1666.

" Musique, in which my utmost luxury still lies."—
LETTER *of Nov.* 22, 1674.

LONDON
SMITH, ELDER, & CO., 15 WATERLOO PLACE
1903

Printed by BALLANTYNE, HANSON & Co
At the Ballantyne Press.

TO THE MEMBERS

OF

THE PEPYS CLUB

The Author and Publishers desire to acknowledge the courtesy of the Corporation of Trinity House in allowing the use of their Plate of the Portrait of Samuel Pepys.

PREFACE

THE following pages are based upon materials which have long been accumulating. Last January I put some of this matter into shape for three lectures delivered at the Royal Institution, and it occurred to me that as this year is the bicentenary of Pepys' death, it might be interesting to give more permanent shape to a sketch of the various points at which he touched the music of his time. Pepys was a many-sided man, and here only one side of him is treated, though that not the least interesting nor the least dear to himself. I feel, also, that to view him from this standpoint is a good corrective to the ordinary estimate of him as only too true a representative of his age.

For valuable assistance in planning out

PREFACE

the book and preparing it for the press, I am much indebted to my son, Mr. R. T. Bridge, of Charterhouse. I have quoted considerably from the complete edition of the Diary, which has laid all students of Pepys under a heavy obligation to Mr. Wheatley, and I must express my thanks to the authorities of Magdalen College, Cambridge, for allowing me to inspect the interesting contents of the Pepysian library, and to make a copy of "Beauty Retire." Lastly, I have to thank Mr. Arthur Hill, of New Bond Street, for drawing my attention to many interesting entries in the State Papers.

J. F. B.

The Cloisters,
    Westminster Abbey.

CONTENTS

APPENDIX

"BEAUTY RETIRE," SONG BY S. PEPYS

ix

" Being in many ways a very ordinary person, he has yet placed himself before the public eye with such a fulness and such an intimacy of detail, as might be envied by a genius like Montaigne. Not then for his own sake only, but as a character in a unique position, endowed with a unique talent, and shedding a unique light upon the lives of the mass of mankind, he is surely worthy of prolonged and patient study."

R. L. STEVENSON, *Men and Books.*

SAMUEL PEPYS

LOVER OF MUSIQUE

CHAPTER I

A MUSICAL ENTHUSIAST

"Musique is the thing of the world that I love most." This is how Samuel Pepys expresses his sentiments on the famous occasion when he had been singing with his wife and her maid, Mercer, in the garden, and when, as he tells us, "coming in, I find my wife plainly dissatisfied with me, that I can spend so much time with Mercer, teaching her to sing, and could never take the pains with her. Which I acknowledge ; but it is because that the girl do take musique mighty readily, and she do not, and musique is the thing of the world that I love most."

SAMUEL PEPYS

The interest with which students of history have perused the pages of Pepys may certainly be imitated by all lovers of music. The period of the Diary and of the later life of Pepys is one in which the music of England made a great advance. For one thing it embraced the life of our greatest composer, Henry Purcell, with his wonderful activity and great achievements in opera and in cathedral and chamber music. We should expect to find in the writings of the observant diarist much interesting information concerning the musical life and art of his time, and in this expectation we shall not be disappointed. Not only in the pages of the immortal Diary, but fortunately in the letters and records of the thirty-three years which elapsed between the close of the Diary and the death of the diarist (1669–1703), music looms very large. It is "still his utmost luxury" (1674), and at a much later time he writes: "Music was never of more use to me than it is now."

But this love of music was by no means the blind admiration of one who knows little about it. It will be found that besides enthusiasm Pepys possessed a fair knowledge of music to which he was constantly adding, and he had undoubtedly a very acute musical ear. This is proved by an account he gives us of an incident occurring at a dinner at Clothworkers' Hall: "Our entertainment very good," he says, "a brave Hall, good company, and very good music, where among other things I was pleased that I could find out a man by his voice, whom I had never seen before, to be the one that sang behind the curtaine formerly at Sir W. Davenent's Opera." As the opera alluded to was performed probably three or four years before this entry, this was something of a feat. That he remembered the tone of a man's voice whom he had never seen and that he recognised the singer by it, is good evidence of Pepys' musical ability.

Besides this natural ability, Pepys possessed good judgment and, on the whole, a fairly unbiassed mind. He knew well the leading musicians of the day, he played various instruments, he studied singing, he attended the services at the Chapel Royal, at

St. Paul's, at Westminster (on one occasion he actually sang in the choir at the Abbey!), and at Windsor, making acute and often amusing comments upon the various choirs and organists. He purchased and, what was more, perused the best theoretical works of the day, both English and foreign, and he tried his hand at composition with very fair success in the case of his often quoted song, "Beauty Retire."

Almost every page of the Diary bears witness to his genuine love of music. He sings through a whole song by Lawes before he goes to church; and when he goes a journey he carries his beloved pipe—not a tobacco pipe, but a flageolet—in his pocket. Even on such an errand as that of escorting King Charles II. back to his kingdom—for which duty Pepys, with others, journeyed to The Hague—he carried his flageolet with him, and tells us the following incident which took place on his landing in Holland: "The rest of the company got a coach by themselves; Mr. Creed and I went in the fore part of a coach wherein were two very pretty

4

ladies, very fashionable, and with black patches, who very merrily sang all the way, and that very well, and were very free to kiss the two blades that were with them. I took out my flageolette and piped, but in piping I dropped my rapier-stick; but when I came to the Hague, I sent my boy back again for it, and he found it, for which I did give him 6d., but some horses had gone over it and broke the scabbard."

It is of course impossible to quote all the musical allusions made by Pepys; he is so observant that he puts down the most minute points, and nothing, however small in detail or simple in performance, escapes his ear. Thus, in one place he complains of the position of the band in the theatre, "sounding under the very stage, there is no hearing of the basses at all, nor very well of the trebles." This is the criticism of a man who evidently discovered a weak spot in the musical arrangements, and was able to define it. Yet on the very next page he writes with equal interest and enthusiasm of his blackbird, which woke him up at four in the morning, "and whistles as well as ever I heard any."

Not satisfied with learning music himself, Pepys was determined that those about him should also be musicians; and great pains he took to carry out his wishes. He began with his wife, and early in the Diary we find the entry: "Some time I spent this morning beginning to teach my wife some scale in music, and found her apt beyond imagination." But alas! poor Mrs. Pepys did not always get such praise from her husband; and there is a sad entry later on which ought to be read while this praise of her early efforts is fresh in the mind: "Before dinner making my wife to sing. Poor wretch! her ear is so bad that it made me angry, till the poor wretch cried to see me so vexed at her, that I think I shall not discourage her so much again, but will endeavour to make her understand sounds and do her good that way." Even his wife, however, shone sometimes by comparison with worse singers. Thus we read in a famous passage: "But, Lord, how did I persuade myself to ask Betty Turner to sing? To see what a beast she is for singing—not one single note in tune—so that but for the experiment I would not for 40s. hear her sing again, worse than my wife a thousand times, so that it do a little reconcile me to her."

Pepys had a great idea of making Mrs. Pepys musical, both for his own sake and for her "encouragement." His sudden resolutions must have often taken Mrs. Pepys somewhat aback. Witness his desire to make her learn a wind instrument. "To the King's House to see 'the Virgin *Massinger and Dekker* Martyr,' the first time it hath been acted a great while, and it is mighty pleasant; not that the play is worth much, but it is finely acted by Becke Marshall. But that which did please me beyond anything in the whole world was the wind - musique when the angel comes down, which is so sweet that it ravished me, and indeed, in a word, did wrap up my soul so that it made me really sick, just as I have formerly been when in love with my wife; that neither then, nor all the evening

7

going home, and at home, I was able to think of any thing, but remained all night transported, so as I could not believe that ever any music hath that real command over the soul of a man as this did upon me; and makes me resolve to practise wind-musique, and to make my wife do the like." · The "wind-musique" practised was the flageolet, for this instrument is mentioned very early in connection with Mrs. Pepys' musical studies.

With regard to her singing-lessons, " I come home," says Pepys, "and find Mr. Goodgroome, my wife's singing-master, and there I did soundly rattle him for neglecting her so much as he hath done—she not having learned three songs these three months and more." Another singing-master was engaged to teach her songs at the fixed price of 10s. a song. She mastered the flageolet, for Pepys writes that he played on it with his wife, "which she now does very prettily," and eventually that " she do outdo therein whatever I expected of her." Sometimes, however, Pepys rather grudged the money that he paid for music; "long with Mr. Berkenshaw in the morning at my musique practice, finishing my song 'Gaze not on Swans,' which pleases me well, and I did give him £5 for this month or five weeks that he hath taught me, which is a great deal of money and troubled me to part with it." This Berkenshaw was the author of certain rules of composition which he evidently imparted to Pepys, who writes: "Up and while I staid for the barber, tried to compose a duo of Counterpoint; and I think it will do very well, it being by Mr. Berkenshaw's rule." This rule was also known to Evelyn, who in the previous year records a visit "to London—a concert of excellent musicians, especially one Mr. Berkenshaw, that rare artist who invented a mathematical way of composure very extraordinary, true as to the exact rules of art, but without much harmonie."

The Diary, too, is full of allusions to the musical powers of Pepys' friends. They, no more than his wife, escaped criticism. On one occasion he heard a Mr. Pickering beginning to play a bass part upon the viall, and he "did it so like a fool that I was ashamed of him." A very different report is given of Mr. North (brother of the well-known Roger North), who was on board ship with Pepys when they went to escort the King from The Hague; "he seems to be a fine gentleman, and at night did play his part exceeding well at first sight."

So, too, the earliest musical allusions in the Diary refer to gatherings with friends at taverns. At the Half-Moon Pepys "found the Captain and Mrs. Billingsby, and Newman a barber, where we were very merry, and had the young man who plays so well upon the Welsh Harp. Billingsby paid for all." Again, at the Green Dragon on Lambeth Hill he "ventured with good success upon things at first sight, and after that played upon my flageolet."

It is interesting to note that the diarist at one point endeavours to throw off somewhat the great attraction which music had for him. He feared it would interfere with his work, and there are two entries which show a spirit of mild asceticism not without parallel in his famous vows against the theatre and wine. In February 1663 he writes : " I played also, which I have not done this long time before upon any instrument, and at last broke up, and I to my office a little while, being fearful of being too much taken with musique, for fear of returning to my old dotage thereon, and so neglect my business as I used to do." And again in April : " This morning Mr. Hunt, the instrument maker, brought me home a Base Viale to see whether I like it, which I do not very well ; besides, I am under a doubt whether I had best buy one yet or no because of spoiling my present mind and love of business." This frame of mind was not very lasting, for exactly a week after this entry we find he spent " all the afternoon fiddling upon my viallin (which I have not done for many a day)." The continuation of this entry perhaps explains his return to his musical love, for he tells us that he fiddled while Ashwell (Mrs. Pepys' maid, who was very musical) " danced above in my upper

11

best chamber, which is a rare room for music." There seems to have been no more thought of giving up music; on the contrary, he teaches Ashwell the ground of time and other things on the tryangle,[1] and he adversely criticises the playing of Mrs. Turner's daughter, presumably sister to the singer who tried him so much. " But, Lord," he says, "it was enough to make any man sick to hear her—yet I was forced to commend her highly." Even in those days apparently criticism was not always candid.

[1] Probably a triangular spinet, not the familiar instrument of to-day.

CHAPTER II

SOME MUSICAL CONTEMPORARIES

As was natural, Pepys knew many of the leading musicians of his time. Of these the earliest mentioned in the Diary are Matthew Lock and Purcell. This latter was the father of the much more famous Henry Purcell, who alas! is not mentioned in the Diary, nor, so far as can yet be ascertained, in any of Pepys' writings. But the younger Purcell was but eleven years of age when the Diary closed, and had not as yet made any figure in the musical world.

It is possible, and indeed probable, that Pepys was brought into contact in later years with Henry Purcell's elder brother. In the Captain Purcell, whom he met at Tangier, we may well see the Lieut.-Colonel Purcell who served under Rooke at the taking of Gibraltar, and under the Prince of Hesse at its memorable defence, and who is buried in the chancel of Wytham Church, near Oxford. The fact also that a copy of Purcell's Sonatas, published by subscription in 1683, is in the Pepysian library, shows that Pepys appreciated the genius who was then organist of the Abbey. Indeed, it is impossible to doubt that he must have been a friend of Purcell, seeing that he knew his father, the elder Purcell, and was on intimate terms with so many of the musicians of Purcell's youth.

With Matthew Lock, then, and the elder Purcell, described as "Master of Musick," Mr. Pepys went to the Coffee House, into a room next the water, and had variety of brave Italian and Spanish songs, and a canon for eight voices which Mr. Lock had lately made on these words, "Domine salvum fac Regem" —an admirable thing—says our enthusiastic critic. Lock was evidently preparing to welcome the restored monarchy, for Charles II. landed within three months, and Lock eventually became composer to the King, some of his music for "sagbutts and cornets"

being played in the royal progress from the
Tower to Whitehall on the day before the
Coronation. The diarist elsewhere refers
to Lock's instrumental music as follows:
"After that W. Howe and I went to play
two trebles in the great cabin below, which
my Lord hearing, after supper he called for
our instruments, and played a set of Lock's,
two trebles and a base, and that being done,
he fell to singing of a song made upon the
Rump, with which he pleased himself well,
to the tune of 'The Blacksmith.'" (This
tune was also known by the name of "Green
Sleeves," and is referred to in *Merry Wives
of Windsor*, ii. 1: "I would have sworn his
disposition would have gone to the truth of
his words; but they do no more adhere and
keep place together, than the Hundredth
Psalm to the tune of 'Green Sleeves.'")

Lock seems to have been somewhat of a
Progressive in music. Indeed Roger North,
the author of the famous Autobiography,
says of him, "he sacrificed the old style
for the modes of his time," and complains of
"his theatricall way." This is borne out by

15

THE BLACKSMITH;

OR,

GREEN SLEEVES AND PUDDING PIES

The Dancing Master, 7th Ed., 1686.

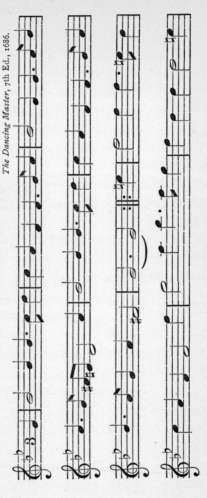

an incident to which Pepys gives a casual reference. Lock had set a Kyrie in an original way, giving different music to each response. This when sung at the Chapel Royal did not meet with the approval of the choir, who seem to have given a very bad rendering of it. Lock at once published it, and prefixed to it a preface entitled " Modern Church Music, Preaccused, Censured, and Obstructed in its performance before His Majesty 1st of April, 1666. Vindicated by its Author, Matthew Locke." Pepys in September 1667 writes : "Spent all the afternoon, Pelling, Howe, and I and my boy, singing of Locke's response to the 10 Commandments which he hath sett very finely, and was a good while since sung before the King, and spoiled in the performance ; which occasioned the printing them, and are excellent good." But for all this the Kyrie was not performed again at the Royal Chapel. Lock was a notable controversialist, and in the heat of conflict did not stop to choose his language. A certain Mr. Salmon roused his anger by a scheme for simplifying musical notation, and by hinting that the opposition to it came from music-teachers who, by prolonging the time required for lessons, wished to make as much as possible out of their pupils. In the course of his reply Mr. Lock says: " Had I been ' purblind,' ' copper-nos'd,' ' sparrow-mouthed,' ' goggle-eyed,' ' hunchbacked ' or the like (ornaments which the best of my antagonists are adorned with), what work would there have been with me ! "

But the greatest of the musicians mentioned in the Diary was undoubtedly Henry Lawes. Born in 1595, he became at the age of thirty a gentleman of the Chapel Royal, and later " a gentleman of the private music to King Charles I." It was no doubt in this capacity that he set the following words to music. The song was included in a masque entitled " The Royal Slave," which was acted before Charles I. and his queen at Oxford. The words were strangely prophetic of the King's tragic end—

> " Come from the dungeon to the throne
> To be a king, and strait be none ;
> Reign then awhile that thou may'st be

LOVER OF MUSIQUE

Fitter to fall by majesty.
So beasts for sacrifice we feed,
First they are crowned, and then they bleed."

Lawes's great claim on the gratitude of posterity is his share in the production of "Comus." Possibly Milton had become acquainted with Lawes through their common love for music. At any rate, when Lawes, on Michaelmas night, 1634, had to provide a masque to be performed at Ludlow before his patron, the Earl of Bridgewater, it was to the young Milton (then aged twenty-five) that he turned. In the actual representation Lawes set the songs to music and himself performed the part of the Attendant Spirit, and he is no doubt alluded to in the words—

"But first I must put off
These my sky robes spun out of Iris' woof,
And take the weeds and likeness of a swain,
That to the service of this house belongs,
Who with his soft pipe, and smooth-dittied song,
Well knows to still the wild winds when they roar,
And hush the waving woods."

Some musical historians have expressed surprise at the admiration with which Lawes was regarded by the great men of his time. Waller, for instance, in some verses inscribed to him, says—

> " Verse makes heroick virtue live
> But you can life to verses give."

The explanation is to be seen in the special characteristic which distinguished Lawes's vocal music—namely, careful attention to the sense and rhythm of the words. This quality is dwelt upon by Milton in his "Sonnet to Mr. H. Lawes on the Publishing his Airs"—

> " Harry, whose tuneful and well-measured song
> First taught our English music how to span
> Words with just note and accent, not to scan
> With Midas' ears, committing short and long."

As Sir Hubert Parry has expressed it: "The songs for 'Comus' show an artistic intention in the sincerity with which the composer endeavoured to follow the rhythm and accent of the poetry rather than to make merely pleasant little tunes."

In keeping with this attention to the meaning of the words was the indignation which Lawes felt and expressed with those who, being quite ignorant of Italian, yet had praise for no songs in any other language. In one of his prefaces he tells the following story: "Not long since some young gentlemen who were not untravelled, hearing some songs I had set to Italian words publickly sung by excellent voices, concluded these songs were begotten in Italy, and said (too loud) 'they would fain hear such songs to be made by an Englishman.' But (to meet with this humour of lusting after novelties) a friend of mine told some of that company 'that a rare new book was come from Italy, which taught the reason why an Eighth was the sweetest of all chords in Musick. Because (said he) Jubal who was Founder of Musick was the Eighth man from Adam,' and this went down as current as that my songs came from Italy."

With the same object in view—that of ridiculing an ignorant admiration for what was foreign just because it was foreign—Lawes wrote his so-called Italian song "Tavola" (*i.e.* "table" or "index"). The music of this is charming, the bright, lively opening and the expressive recitative in the middle being alike beautiful; but the words are nothing more or less than an index to a collection of Italian songs, together with the headings denoting the number of voices for which they are set. The following is a translation of the words :—

> In that frozen heart,
> For one voice.
> My lady weeps,
> If your eyes,
> For two voices.
> Oh ever when thou seek'st to save me,
> I fight and scorn.
> May not the unhappy one believe,
> Alas! with former lights.
> What anguish from the pallid lip.
> Thus my life,
> For three voices.

This is Lawes's account of the origin of the song, as given in the preface to his first book of Ayres: "I never loved to set or sing words which I do not understand; and where I cannot, I desired help of others who were able to interpret.

But this present generation is so sated with what's native, that nothing takes their eares but what's sung in a language which commonly they understand as little as they do the Music. And to make them a little sensible of this ridiculous humour, I took a Table or Index of old Italian songs (for one, two, and three voices), and this Index (which read together makes a strange medley of nonsense), I set to a varied ayre, and gave out that it came from Italy, whereby it hath passed for a rare Italian song. This very song I have here printed." It would be interesting to know what were the feelings of those who had ignorantly admired this mock-Italian song when they saw the same in print in Lawes's " Book of Ayres and Dialogues."

Lawes died in October 1662, and therefore we need not expect to find much reference by Pepys to personal acquaintance with him. He does, however, in December 1660, record that he entered two songs by Lawes into his song-book " to which I have got Mr. Child to set the base to the

Theorbo "; and a little later he mentions
that Mr. Child, after promising to prick him
some lessons on the theorbo, went away " to
see Henry Lawes who lies very sick. I to
the Abby and walked there seeing the great
confusion of people that come there to hear
the Organs." Pepys also frequently sang
Lawes's music ; for instance, he tells us that
one " Lord's Day " he sang Orpheus' hymn
before he went to church.

During the time of the Commonwealth,
Henry Lawes maintained himself by teaching,
and lived to compose some of the music for
Charles II.'s Coronation. He died in October 1662, and was buried in the Cloisters
at Westminster. His later life was spent in
the Almonry, where was living at the same
time the elder Purcell. There can be no
doubt that Lawes must have known the
great Henry as a child, and it is significant
that in Purcell's (supposed) first composition, a little trio, "Sweet Tyranness," written
while he was still a boy, we find a phrase
borrowed from Lawes's "Comus" music.
Doubtless Purcell had often heard the

composer play it in their quaint old houses at Westminster.

Pepys also was familiar with the music of Henry Lawes's brother William. This musician led a more adventurous life than his brother, and in the end was killed fighting for his king at the siege of Chester, having refused to occupy a post of comparative safety to which a friendly general had appointed him. There is a touching reference to his death in a preface by his brother Henry to a collection of Psalms by both of them. "These following compositions," he says, "of mine and my Brother's I have been much importuned to send to the press, and should not easily have been persuaded to it now (especially in these dissonant times), but to do a right (or at least show my love) to the memory of my brother, unfortunately lost in these unnaturall warres,—yet lies in the bed of honour, and expired in the service and defence of the King his master." Pepys mentions his music several times, and the following entry is a type of many : "After all this he called for the fiddles and books, and we two and W. Howe and Mr. Childe did sing and play some Psalms of Will Lawes and some songs."

The name of Pelham Humfrey recalls an interesting and notable figure. Pepys in November 1663 tells us that he went to the Royal Chapel, and says: "The anthem was good after sermon, being the 51st Psalm made for 5 voices by one of Captain Cooke's[1] boys, a pretty boy." This anthem we still possess, and with reference to it Pepys continues: "Here I first perceived that the King (Charles II.) is a little musical and kept good time with his hand all along the Anthem." But indeed, unfortunately for English art, the King had very distinct views on music. He could not endure the sobriety of the English music, but was an ardent admirer of the lighter French style. Pepys tells us in one place that "the King did

---

[1] This Henry Cooke, organist of the Chapel Royal, had obtained his captain's commission in 1642, during the Civil War, and retained his military title for the rest of his life. Pepys says of him, "a vain coxcomb he is, though he sings and composes so well." He died in 1672.

put a great affront upon Singleton's musique,
he bidding them stop, and bade the French
musique play, which my Lord says do much
outdo all ours." The king did more than
this. He sent the young Pelham Humfrey
abroad to study under Lully, the great
French dramatic composer. We can understand that to Humfrey this would open a
new world. Hitherto his horizon had been
bounded by the ecclesiastical music of the
Chapel Royal, and the early attempts at so-
called English opera by Lawes, Lock, and
others. But now he would make acquaintance with the operas which Lully was producing in France. On his return Pepys
invited him with others to his house, and
has left us his impressions of the genius
home from his continental tour. November
15, 1667: "Home and there I find as I
expected Mr. Cæsar and little Pelham Humfrey lately returned from France, and is an
absolute Monsieur as full of form and con-
fidence and vanity, and disparages everything
and everybody's skill but his own. The
truth is, everybody says he is very able,

but to hear how he laughs at all the King's Musick here, as Blagrave and others, that they cannot keep time nor tune nor understand anything; and that Grebus the Frenchman, the King's Master of the Musick, how he understands nothing nor can play on any instrument and so cannot compose; and that he will give him a lift out of his place; and that he and the king are mighty great. I had a good dinner for them, as a venison pasty and some fowl, and after dinner we did play—he on the Theorbo, Mr. Cæsar on his French lute, and I on the viol—but made but mean musique, nor do I see that this Frenchman do so much wonders on the Theorbo, but without question, he is a good musician, but his vanity do offend me." The Grebus here mentioned is better known as Louis Grabu, and of him we shall speak later.

On the next day Pepys again came across Humfrey, this time at Court. "To White Hall, where there is to be a performance of Music of Pelham's before the King. The company not come; but I did go into the

Music Room where were Captain Cooke and many others, and here I did hear the best and the smallest Organ go that ever I saw in my life, and such a one as by the grace of God I will have the next year, if I continue in this condition, whatever it cost me." (The organ at the Chapel Royal at Whitehall was probably built by Father Smith, and we have a warrant of the year 1671, " to the Commissioners of the Customs to permit —— Smith, the King's organ-maker, to import several tools and implements for the repair of the organ in the Chapel Royal at Whitehall.") Later on he went " into the theatre-room and there heard both the vocall and instrumentall music, where the little fellow (Pelham Humfrey) stood keeping time, but for my part I see no great matter but quite the contrary in both sorts of Music. . . . The composition I believe is very good, but no more of delightfulness to the eare or understanding but what is very ordinary."

Humfrey prospered in the Royal service, for in the State Papers for the year 1668, we have a " warrant to pay Pelham Humphrys, Musician in ordinary on the lute in place of Nich. Sawyer, deceased, £40 yearly, and £16. 2s. 6d. for livery." All this success was not calculated to improve the musician's modesty, and we find Pepys again describing him as a "swaggering young handsome gentleman," and contrasting him with his companion, Mr. Monteith, "a sober citizen merchant." Humfrey, he said, sang "with great skill, the other no skill but a good voice and a good basse, but used only to tavern tunes; and so I spent all this evening till 11 at night singing with them till I was tired of them because of the swaggering fellow, tho' the girl Mercer did mightily commend him before to me." Later in the same year Pepys, who has been after an espinette at Deptford, finds on his return home Humfrey and others in the garden, "and there had most excellent Musick late, in the dark, with great pleasure."

Pelham Humfrey is most widely known at the present day as the composer of the so-called Grand Chant. But his highest title to fame consists in his having been a master of Henry Purcell. In July 1672 he was made organist of the Chapel Royal in succession to his own master, Captain Cooke. In the choir may still have been Purcell, at this time fourteen years old, who was no doubt an eager listener to the "new effects" which Humfrey introduced. The two, master and pupil, even composed an anthem conjointly, with the title, " By the waters of Babylon." To Purcell, we may believe, he handed on the torch of his own inspiration, for he himself never fulfilled his early promise, but died at Windsor at the early age of twenty-seven. The somewhat sweeping assertion has been made that he was "the first of our ecclesiastical composers who had the least idea of musical pathos and expression of the words." Without going so far as this we must certainly admit that he is one of the first to show that feeling for dramatic expression and correct accentuation which is so prominent in Purcell and of which Henry Lawes was the undoubted originator.

It is perhaps worth mentioning here that the king did approve of one form of English music. On New Year's Eve, 1662, Pepys went to a ball at Whitehall, and gives us a list of notables present. He goes on to say : " And they danced the Bransle. After that the King led a lady a single Coranto; and then the rest of the lords, one after another, other ladies; very noble it was, and great pleasure to see. Then to country dances, the King leading the first, which he called for, which was, says he, ' Cuckolds all awry,' the old dance of England." The Bransle or Brawl, as we are told, was an old round dance, in which the performers joined hands in a circle, and in which kissing the whole of the ladies, by each of the gentlemen in turn, was one of the chief features.

Another friend of the diarist was Christopher Gibbons, organist of Westminster Abbey, and in connection with him there is an entry of real interest. Gibbons joined Lord Sandwich and another " in playing a good Fancy, to which my Lord is fallen again, and says he cannot endure a merry tune, which is a strange turn of his humour, after he has for two or three years

BRANSLE, OR BRAWL

Rather fast.

33

c

CUCKOLDS ALL AWRY

34

flung off the practice of Fancies and played only fiddlers' tunes." Students of English musical history will here recognise the course which music took under Charles II. We have seen in connection with Pelham Humfrey that the King "could not endure" the sedate old English style of music, sacred or secular. He established a band of twenty-four violins, ordered symphonies and interludes to be played in the anthems, and did all he could to bring in the French style. No doubt Lord Sandwich had followed the fashion of the Court; but here we find him "flinging off fiddlers' tunes" and returning to the old English Fancy. The Fancy, as a rule, consisted of contrapuntal imitative music, abounding in device and dull in style. Fancies were the usual form of instrumental chamber-music at this time, and were written by all the eminent masters, from Orlando Gibbons to Lock, and even Henry Purcell. They existed before Fugue was endowed with form, and show our composers somewhat heavily feeling their way to the Trios of Purcell and Corelli, and so leading on to the first real landmark of modern chamber music—the string quartette.[1]

Gibbons was evidently in favour with Charles II., for in the State Papers there exists a letter written on July 2, 1663, directing the University of Oxford to confer on him the degree of Doctor of Music. The letter runs as follows:—

To our trusty and welbeloved the Vice-Chancellor, Doctors, Proctors and Masters of the University of Oxford.

Trusty and welbeloved, wee greete you well. Whereas the bearer, Christopher Gibbons, one of the organists of our Chappell Royall, hath from his youth served our Royall father and our selfe, And hath soe well improved himselfe in musique as well in our owne judgement as the judgement of all men well skilled in that science as that he may worthily receave your honer and degree of Doctor

---

[1] In Mr. Wheatley's very complete edition these Fancies are erroneously described as a kind of "light airs," and it is stated that Dr. Hueffer, the late accomplished critic of the *Times*, was "inclined to connect them with the Fantasia." The context, however, shows that they had a graver character than "light airs," and indeed they are a definite species of composition belonging to this period, and perfectly well understood.

36

therein, wee in consideracon of his merritt and fittness thereunto, have thought fitt by these our Letters to recommend him unto you. And to signify our gracious pleasure to be, that he be forthwith admitted and created by you, Doctor in Musique. He performing his exercises and paying all his due fees, any statute or custome whatsoever be contrary notwithstanding.[1]

It is interesting to find that in the case of his "honorary" degree the recipient had yet to write and have performed a musical composition or exercise, and pay the fees.

It may be mentioned that Gibbons served the King's "Royal Father" not only as a musician, but, with his brother musicians, Lawes and Cooke, as a soldier. During the Civil War, we are told (in the State Papers), he went into one of the garrisons. His portrait is in the Examination Schools at Oxford.

[1] State Papers, Domestic, Charles II., vol. 76, No. 13.

CHAPTER III

MORE MUSICAL CONTEMPORARIES

THE composers mentioned in the previous chapter were most distinguished for their vocal writings. In this chapter we include some names more intimately connected with the development of instrumental music and generally in connection with the King's Band.

John Banister is another well-known musician whom the diarist mentions, and indeed many of the flageolet tunes in Greeting's Book, from which Mr. and Mrs. Pepys studied this favourite instrument, were composed by Banister, who himself was a celebrated flageolet player. In conjunction with Pelham Humfrey he set music to the *Tempest*, and this music Pepys refers to when he says, "I did get him to prick me down the notes of the Echo in the *Tempest*, which pleases me mightily."

38

In 1663 he appears to have been appointed leader of the King's band of twenty-four violins on the death of Baltzar, and to have received a further commission to organise a select band of twelve from these violins to play before the King whenever music was required. The warrant for this still exists among the State Papers, and from its intrinsic interest may well be quoted in full.

Whereas wee have beene pleased to appoint our welbeloved servant John Banister to make choice of twelve of our fower and twenty violins, to be a select Band to wait on us, wheresoever there shall be occasion for musique, And that he doe give his attendance on us constantly to receive our commands, and to see that our service be performed by the said twelve persons; And in consideracon of their extraordinary service done and to be done unto us, and the smallenesse of their wages already settled, Wee are willing to augment the same. Our will and pleasure therefore is, That you prepare a Warrant fitt for our royall signature for the payment of six hundred poundes per annum to passe by our Letters of Privy Seale unto the said John Banister, to be by him received at the receipt of our Exchequer for himselfe and twelve of our said violins. And upon receipt thereof to be

equally divided to such persons, as he hath already
made choice of, or shall from time to time for our
said service, And the first payment of the said six
hundred poundes per annum to commence from
the five and twentieth of March, which was in the
yeare of Our Lord one thousand, six hundred sixty
and two. And the arreares that have accrewed
and growne due since the said five and twentieth
of March 1662 to the fower and twentieth day of
June last past to be paid off, And from thenceforth
to be paid quarterly by equall porčons, out of the
Receipt of our Exchequer during our pleasure.
And our further will and pleasure is, That if any
of our said Band of Violins nominated, or to be
nominated, by the said John Banister, Master of
our said Band, shall either neglect practices or performance before us in Consort upon his summons,
or mix in any musique whatsoever otherwise than
for our particular service in our said Band, without
the knowledge and allowance of the said John
Banister, That upon his complaint to the Lord
Chamberlaine of our houshold, such person or
persons so offending shall be discharged from this
our private musicke and such others of our other
twelve violins taken into their roomes for the
performance of this our said particular service, as
our said Lord Chamberlaine shall thinke fitt and
allow of upon the recommendačon of the said John
Banister. And for your soe doeing this shall be

your Warrant. Given at our Court at Whitehall this . . . of July, In the fifteenth yeare of our Reigne.[1]

To the Clerke of our
Signet attending.

This post Banister held for about three years. In February 1667 Pepys tells that he was much put out by the arrival of a Frenchman, named Grabu, to be Master of the King's Music. " Here (at the Duke of York's) they talk also how the King's viallin Bannister is mad that the King hath a Frenchman come to be chief of some part of the King's Musique, at which the Duke of York made great mirth." The arrival of this Frenchman was a serious matter for Banister, for from some cause or other Grabu supplanted him as the head of this select band of twelve. Even before this appointment was conferred upon Grabu, he seems to have had authority, as the warrant for his new appointment runs thus : " Our

[1] State Papers, Domestic, Charles II., July 1663, vol. 77, No. 40.

will, etc., that you give order for the swear-
ing —— Grabu, our *Director in Ordinary*, as
master of our English Chamber Musicke."
This is dated November 12, 1666, two or
three months before the above-quoted re-
mark of Pepys.

It has been pretty generally stated that
Banister owed his dismissal to an injudicious
observation made in the hearing of the King,
" that he preferred English violins to the
French." This may have been one reason,
but it would seem that Banister's conduct
in financial matters was not above reproach,
and may have had something to do with his
removal from office. The following amusing
petition of the Band gives us much insight
into his failings in this respect.

Wee the band of violins now under the direction of Monsr. Grabu, Master of his Majesties
musique, doe humbly represent to your Lordshipp
—That it was his Majesties will and pleasure to
give unto his Band of Violins late under the direction of John Banister 600*l.* per annum for doeing
extraordinary service. This John Banister under-
takes it for himselfe and demanded of the Com-

pany 20*l*. a peice, or all the arreares that was due to them from the Queenes comeing in untill Michaelmas 1663, which, if we refused, hee swore wee should be turned out of the Band, for said hee, I am to carry upp the names to morrow morning to the Councell Chamber, and they that will not doe this, their names shall be left out, and others put in : But instead of putting in ours or others into a Privy Seale to receive the said 600*l*., hee onely put in his owne name unknowne to us, soe wee consented to give him all that was due to us before that time, for 20*l*. a peice could not be raysed by us and in doeing this hee did promise that wee should have 10*l*. a peice every quarter of him, whether he did receive it or not, and wee should begin from Michaelmas 1663, but unknowne to us hee had gott it granted a yeare and an halfe before, and since this Agreement he hath received 950*l*. for this Augmentation, of which said 950*l*. some have received of him 20*l*., some 10*l*., and one but 7*l*. 10*s*. and others more. And in 1663 wee played to the Queenes dancing which was her Birth Day, and wee presumed to speake to the Lord Chesterfield to speake for our accustomed fee, and the Lord Chesterfield spake to the Queene for us, but the Queens Treasurer being by, told the Queene, we had received great summes of money already, about 230*l*., which Mr. Banister keepes from us, as his owne right by giving him

our arreares, and setting our hands to it, but it was
that hee should performe his bargaine with us.
The Queene hearing hee had such a summe of
money was very angry, but wee never did speake
before, and if we had not spoke then, wee never
had knowne of the money, for Mr. Banister would
not suffer us to looke after any money that is due
to us, hee sayes, how dare wee doe it. That the
said Banister received 50*l*. from the Queenes
Majestie at the Bath, and paid to those that
attended only 5*l*. each, keeping 20*l*. for himselfe.
Also a person of honour giving us 10*l*. in gould
for attendance, the said Banister kept fower peeces
for himselfe. And 20*l*. he received from the
Duke of Buckingham for us, of which wee never
had one penny, besides severall other things of that
nature. And this last birthday of the Queenes
he gets the fee of 10*l*. into his hands, and gives
money to some, and to others not a penny, neither
did hee waite on the Queene himselfe. Likewise
Mr. Banister hath kept sometimes five or six of us
out of wayting, according as hee is pleased or dis-
pleased, and three of us he hath turned out of his
Band, his Majesties pleasure not being knowne
therein, nor the Lord Chamberlaines, by this
meanes, hee thinkes to put all our arreares in his
owne purse, whereby the King's service is abused,
and his poore servants utterly ruyned. Wee therefore most humbly desire that your Lordshipp would

be pleased to order the Caveat to be taken off, that soe the Seale may passe. And if any objecčon be made by the said Banister, wee are ready and willing humbly to submitt to what your Lordshipp shall please to order therein.[1]

At the same time Banister seems to have sent in a counter-petition to the King claiming certain arrears, for we have a paper in which Charles directs an inquiry to be held and a report to be made to him. In the meantime the salaries and arrears for the special band are not to be paid to Grabu. Finally, the report was unfavourable to Banister, and it is directed that the salaries and arrears shall be duly paid to Grabu as Master of the Music, and the Lord Chamberlain adds that he has determined to " see it justly distributed hereafter."

The wording of this report shows that Grabu was already Master of the Music, and that these matters referred to his new appointment as head of the select band in place of Banister.

[1] State Papers, Domestic, Charles II., March 29, 1667, vol. 195, No. 62.

My Lord,—The grant of the Privy Seale which Bannester had for a particular Band of Violins, was by his Majesties especiall comand given to Mons. Grabu, Master of the Musick; and a stop was made, upon Bannesters petition, that hee might receave the arreares due in the Exchequer. But the whole Band of Violins complayning severall times that Banister had wronged them in their share and dividend; I did thinke it fitt upon hearing all parties and by the consent of all, to order that the Master of the Musick should receave it, and that I would see it justly distributed hereafter : wherewith I acquainted his Majestie, and his Majestie was well pleased therewith and comanded that the Master of the Musick should receave it, and should have his Privy Seale pass as it is drawne.

Thus I rest.   Your Lo^pps humble servant,

E. Manchester.[1]

Aug. 4 1667.

Banister is notable as having been the first musician to give public concerts in London. From the *London Gazette* of the time we get such notices as the following : " Dec. 30, 1672. These are to give notice, that at

---

[1] State Papers, Domestic, Charles II., Aug. 4th, 1667, vol. 212, No. 56.

Mr. John Banister's house (now called the Musick - school) over against the George tavern in White Fryers, this present Monday, will be musick performed by excellent masters, beginning precisely at 4 of the clock in the afternoon, and every afternoon for the future, precisely at the same hour." White Fryers was close to the spot which is now covered by the Guildhall School of Music. These concerts were given at intervals till 1678, in which year the last notice of them appears: "Nov. 18. On Thursday next, the 22nd of this instant November, at the Musick-school in Essex-buildings, over-against St. Clement's church in the Strand, will be continued a consort of vocal and instrumental musick, beginning at five of the clock every evening, composed by Mr. John Banister." In the following year Banister died, and the concerts came to an end. Roger North, an amateur of even greater knowledge than Pepys, has left us in his "Memoires of Musick" an interesting account of these concerts. Of Banister he writes: "He procured a large room in

Whitefriars, near the Temple back gate, and made a large raised box for the musicians, whose modesty required curtains. The room was rounded with seats and small tables, alehouse fashion. One shilling was the price, and call for what you pleased; there was very good music, for Banister found means to procure the best bands in town, and some voices to come and perform there, and there wanted no variety of humour, for Banister himself (*inter alia*) did wonders upon a flageolet to a thorough bass, and the several masters had their solos. This continued full one winter, and more I remember not." North, however, did not fully approve of the arrangements at concerts during this period, and passes the following sound criticisms upon them. This system as begun by Banister was, he says, "called the Musickmeeting; and all the quality and beau monde repaired to it, but the plan of this project was not so well laid as it ought to have been, for the time of their beginning was inconsistent with the park and the playhouses, which had a stronger attraction. And what was worse, the masters undertakers were a rope of sand, not under the rule or order of any person, and everyone forward to advance his own talents, and spiteful to each other, and out of emulation substracting their skill in performing ; all which together scandalized the company and poisoned the entertainment. Besides the whole was without design or order ; for one master brings a concert with fugues, another shows his gifts in a solo upon the violin, another sings, and then a famous lutinist comes forward, and in this manner changes followed each other, with a full cessation of the musick between every one, and a gabble and bustle while they changed places ; whereas all entertainments of this kind ought to be projected as a drama, so as all the members shall uninterruptedly follow in order, and having a true connexion, set off each other. It is no wonder that the play-houses got ground, and as they ordered the matter, soon routed this Musick-meeting."

Banister did not long survive his friend and collaborateur, Pelham Humfrey, for he died in 1679, and was buried not far from Humfrey in the cloisters of Westminster Abbey, where a small monument to his memory may still be seen.

Grabu became a prominent figure in Court music and Pepys has several references to him, but not as a rule of very complimentary character. For instance, on October 1, 1667, he writes: "To White Hall, and there in the Boarded Gallery did hear the Musick with which the King is presented this night by Mons. Grebus, the Master of his musick; both instrumentall—I think 24 violins—and vocal; an English song upon Peace. But God forgive me! I never was so little pleased with a concert of musick in my life. The manner of setting of words and repeating them out of order, and that with a number of voices, makes me sick, the whole design of vocal musick being lost by it. Here was a great press of people; but I did not see many pleased with it, only the instrumental Musick he had brought by practice to play very just." We must not take this criticism too seriously, for Pepys did not admire any very elaborate music, and in one entry says : " I am more and more confirmed that singing with many voices is not singing, but a sort of instrumental musique, the sense of the words being lost by not being heard, and especially as they set them with Fugues of words, one after another, whereas singing properly I think should be but with one or two voices at most and the counterpoint." Grabu is chiefly interesting to us from his connection with Dryden. The latter wrote the libretto of an opera entitled " Albion and Albanius," and out of respect, no doubt, for the French sympathies of the Court in matters musical, got Grabu to write the music for it.

The preface in which the Frenchman commends his work to King James II. is so interesting that no apology is necessary for giving it in full.

To the King.

SIR,—After the shipwrack of all my fairest hopes and expectations on the death of the late King, my master, your royal brother of ever blessed memory, the only consolation I have left is that the labour I have bestowed on this musical representation has partly been employ'd in paying my most humble duty to the person of your most sacred Majesty. The happy invention of the poet furnished me with that occasion : the feigned misfortune of two persecuted heros was too thin a veil for the moral not to shine through the fable ; the pretended plot and the true conspiracy were no more disguised on the private stage than they were on the public theater of the world. Never were two Princes united more straightly together in common sufferings from ungrateful and rebellious subjects. The nearness of their blood was not greater than the conformity of their fortunes : but the Almighty has received the one to his mercy in Heaven, and rewarded the constancy and obedience of the other here below : Virtue is at last triumphant in both places ; Immortality is actually possessed by one monarch, and the other has the earnest of it in the type of earthly glory. My late gracious master was pleased to encourage this my humble undertaking, and did me the honour to make some esteem of this my part in the performance of it, having more than once condescended to be present at the repetition before it came into the public view. Your majesty has been also pleased to do me the same honour, when it appeared at your theatre in greater splendour and with more advantages of ornament ; and I may be justly proud to own that you gave it the particular grace of your royal protection. As the subject of it is naturally magnificent, it could not but excite my genius and raise it to a greater height, in the composition, even to surpass itself : at least, a virtuous emulation of doing well can never be so faulty but it may be excused by the zeal of the undertaker, who laid his whole strength to the pleasing of a master and a sovereign. The only displeasure which remains with me is that I neither was nor could possibly be furnished with variety of excellent voices to present it to your majesty in its full perfection. Notwithstanding which you have been pleased to pardon this defect, as not proceeding from any fault of mine but only from the scarcity of singers in this Island. So that I have nothing more at this time to beg than the continuance of that patronage, which your princely goodness hath so graciously allowed me : as having no other ambition in the world than that of pleasing you, and the desire of shewing myself on all possible occasions and with the most profound respect to be

Your Majesty's most humble, most obliged, and most obedient servant,

LEWIS GRABU.

In the preface Dryden says of him that his "qualities have raised M. Grabu to a

degree above any man who shall pretend to
be his rival on our stage." The opera, however, was a failure, and Dryden later on
recognised the far greater genius of Grabu's
contemporary, Purcell, and collaborated with
him, first of all in the songs for "Amphi-
tryon," a comedy produced in 1690, and
later in the more important opera of "King
Arthur." After Dryden's panegyric on
Grabu above quoted, it is interesting to find
him speaking of Purcell as one "in whose
person we have at length found an Englishman equal with the best abroad." But in
spite of the general disparagement of Grabu,
some of his music, for instance a sailor's song,
"Medway and Isis," shows that he caught
the spirit of the words; moreover the accompaniment, written for strings and quite
independent of the voice part, is a clear proof
of his knowledge of the orchestra. In one
thing he lamentably failed, the "just accent"
which distinguished Lawes, but this no doubt
was due to his foreign extraction.

Certainly some of the words of the opera
were not calculated to "excite the genius"

of any musician. They were of course exclusively political, as may be gathered from the following lines to be sung by the oddly-assorted pair, Democracy and Zelota—

> *D.* Democracy kept nobles under.
> *Z.* Zeal for the Pulpit roared like thunder.
> *Z.* I trampled on the State.
> *D.* I lorded o'er the Gown.
> *Both.* We both in triumph sate,
> Usurpers of the Crown.

At the house of Lord Brouncker—the first president of the Royal Society, and the translator of and commentator on Descartes' treatise called *Musicæ Compendium*—which seems to have been a meeting-place for musicians, Pepys met the Italian Giovanni Battista Draghi. After that meeting he writes that Draghi "hath composed a play in Italian for the opera which T. Killigrew do intend to have up; and here he did sing one of the acts. He himself is the poet as well as the musician, which is very much, and did sing the whole from the words without any music prickt, and played all along upon a harpsicon most admirably and the composition most excellent." On the death of Matthew Lock, Draghi was appointed organist to the Queen, Catherine of Braganza. But this "excellent and stupendous artist," as Evelyn calls him, did not remain permanently in England, and in the next reign probably returned with the Dowager-Queen to Portugal. Another meeting with Draghi drew from the delighted Pepys a strong profession of the faith that was in him. After saying that all this music interferes with his work, he continues: "But then I do consider that this is all the pleasure I live for in the world, and the greatest I can ever expect in the best of my life, and one thing more, that by hearing this man to-night, and I think Captain Cooke to-morrow, and the quire of Italians on Saturday, I shall be truly able to distinguish which of them pleases me truly best, which I do much desire to know and have good reason and fresh occasion of judging." Here again Pepys proves himself an ardent musician and conscientious critic, desiring the widest experience, and taking this opportunity of comparing chamber music, the English cathedral music, and Italian sacred music.

Another musical friend of Pepys was William Laniere, son of the Nicholas Laniere who wrote the symphonies to several of Ben Jonson's masques. Pepys was on familiar terms with the son, and often met him. Thus on December 6, 1665, he writes: "With my wife walked and Mercer to Mrs. Peirce's, where Captain Rolt and Mrs. Knipp, Mr. Coleman and his wife, and Laneare, Mrs. Worshipp and her singing daughter met. . . . Here the best company for musique I ever was in in my life, and wish I could live and die in it, both for musique and the face of Mrs. Peirce and my wife and Knipp, who is pretty enough; but the most excellent, mad-humoured thing, and sings the noblest that ever I heard in my life, and Rolt, with her, some things together most excellently. I spent the night in extasy almost." A month later we have the following scene, with its melancholy ending: "So

home and find all my good company I had
bespoke, as Coleman and his wife and
Laneare, Knipp and her surly husband;
and good musique we had, and among
other things Mrs. Coleman sang my words
I set of 'Beauty Retire,' and I think it is
a good song, and they praise it mightily.
Then to dancing and supper and mighty
merry till Mr. Rolt come in, whose pain
of the tooth-ake made him no company,
and spoilt ours; so he away, and then my
wife's teeth fell of akeing and she to bed.
So forced to break up all with a good song
and so to bed." Of Laniere's singing Pepys
approved, for he tells us that " Laneare
sings in a melancholy method very well,
and a sober man he seems to be." On
reviewing the year 1665, Pepys includes
Laniere in the small circle of friends
to whom he owes it that he has never
" lived so merrily " as during this plague
time.

It is possible also that we ought to include
the musician Blow among those whom Pepys
mentions, for on August 21, 1667, he

writes: "This morning come two of Captain Cooke's boys, whose voices are broke, and are gone from the Chapel, but have extraordinary skill; and they and my boy, with his broken voice, did sing three parts; their names were Blaew and Loggings; but notwithstanding their skill, yet to hear them sing with their broken voices, which they could not command to keep in tune, would make a man mad—so bad it was." Blow was, we know, in the Chapel Royal choir, and his age at this time was nineteen, so that he may be the same as Blaew with the broken voice.

Besides his professional friends, Mr. Pepys saw much of an amateur, Mr. Hill, in connection with whom there are one or two entries of importance. "Home by water, and there find, as I expected, Mr. Hill and Andrews, and one slovenly and ugly fellow, Seignor Pedro, who sings Italian songs to the theorbo most neatly, and they spent the whole evening in singing the best piece of musique counted of all hands in the world, made by Seignor Charissimi, the famous master in Rome. Fine it was, indeed, and too fine for me to judge of. They have spoke to Pedro to meet us every weeke, and I fear it will grow a trouble to me if we once come to bid judges to meet us, especially idle masters, which do a little displease me to consider." His fears were justified; the presence of the professional made the amateur diffident, and a week later he says of the same party : " Great store of musique we had, but I begin to be weary of having a master with us, for it spoils, methinks, the ingenuity of our practice." Pepys here laid his finger on a fault to which must be attributed some of the decay into which English music soon fell. With this innovation of public concerts, music drifted more and more into the hands of the professional class, and ceased to be the general resource of the many. The same complaint is made by Roger North a few years later. It is from the pages of Pepys that we learn what an important place during this age music took in the daily life of the people.

Pepys soon tired of the professional help

of Signor Pedro, and a little later tells us :
" Thence home, and though late, yet Pedro
being there, he sang a song and parted. I
did give him 5s., but find it burdensome,
and so will break up the meeting."

CHAPTER IV

PEPYS AS VOCALIST AND SINGING-MASTER

IF we could have met Mr. Pepys on one of his little expeditions on Admiralty business to Erith or to Woolwich, we should most probably have found him singing. No doubt as a young man he was what is termed "musical," and had reached a certain degree of proficiency, for we read on December 9, 1660: "This being done I went to chappell" (at Whitehall) "and sat in Mr. Blagrave's pew, and there did sing my part along with another before the King, and with much ease." On the anniversary of Charles I.'s death he marks the day by a song of his own. January 30, 1660: "This morning, before I was up, I fell a-singing of my song, 'Great, good, and just, &c.,' and put myself thereby in mind that this was the fatal day, now ten

years since, his majesty died." [1] The words
of this song were by the Marquis of Mon-
trose, and are worth recalling—

> " Great, good, and just, could I but rate
> My grief with thy too rigid fate,

---

[1] In this reference to the execution of Charles I., Pepys
is a year wrong in his calculation. The King was exe-
cuted on January 30, 1649, and therefore Pepys should
have said " eleven " and not " ten years since." This
would not be worth noticing except for the well-known
fact that both Pepys and Mrs. Pepys made mistakes as
to the date on which they were married. The same trait
also is perhaps to be illustrated by the following curious
piece of evidence which I owe to Dr. Edward Scott of
the British Museum. Pepys always kept as an anniversary the 26th of March, on which day he had once been
cut for the stone. Now among the Sloane MSS. at the
British Museum occur the entries from the books of the
apothecary who supplied Pepys with medicine on that
occasion. The entries are as follows :—

Sloane MS., 1536.

In the margin of f. 63 (which contains a prescrip-
tion) : " before he was cut for ye stone by M^r. Hollyer.

" M^r. Peapes.   D^r. J. M."

And in the margin of f. 63b, opposite another pre-
scription : " to be in rediness when he was cut. For
M^r. Peapes who was cut for ye stone by M^r. Hollier,
March ye 28 (1658) and had a very great stone taken y^t
day from him.

" D^r. J. M.   D^r. G. Jolly."

It may be noticed that in the latter entry the date
given is March 28th *not* 26th, so possibly in this instance
also Pepys had got the date wrong.

I'd weep the world in such a strain
As it should deluge once again.

" But since thy loud-tongued blood demands supplies,
More from Briareus' hands than Argus' eyes,
I'll sing thine obsequies with trumpet sounds,
And write thine epitaph in blood and wounds."

Even at this early stage Pepys was, as ever, critical. " Here Swan," he says, " showed us a ballad to the tune of Mardike which was most incomparably wrote in a printed hand, which I borrowed of him, but the song proved but silly, and so I did not write it out." With the view, however, of becoming really efficient, he engaged a singing-master. In June 1661 he wrote: "This morning came Mr. Goodgroome to me (recommended by Mr. Mage [1]), with whom I agreed presently to give him 20s. entrance, which I then did, and 20s. a month more to teach me to sing, and so we began, and I hope I have come to something in it. His first song is ' La cruda la bella.' "

As soon as he begins to take lessons his criticisms become more frequent, and he him-

[1] Probably Madge, one of the King's Band.

self seems to realise that increased knowledge
has made him more fastidious.   He hears
Mr. Blagrave and his kinswoman sing, but
he notes : " I was not pleased with it, they
singing methought very ill, or else I am
grown worse to please than heretofore."
He was careful, however, occasionally to
conceal his feelings, though they are as usual
not hidden in the faithful Diary.   Thus he
writes : " After supper I made the ladies
sing, and they have been taught, but Lord !
though I was forced to commend them, yet
it was the saddest stuff I ever heard.   However we sat up late, and then I, in the best
chamber like a prince, to bed, and Creed
with me, and being sleepy talked but
little."

Pepys lost no opportunity of practising his
singing.   One Sunday he writes: " Up, and
after being trimmed, alone by water to Erith,
all the way with my song-book singing of
Mr. Lawes's long recitative song in the beginning of his book."   He also records a
charming incident that took place on a
similar expedition by water ; we can see

from it how sociable the diarist was. "*July* 13, 1665.—I by water at night late to Sir G. Carteret's, but there being no one to carry me, I was fain to call a skuller that had a gentleman already in it, and he proved a man of love to musique, and he and I sung together the way down with great pleasure, and an incident extraordinary to be met with." On Sundays, too, his training made him more observant of the music in church. "This morning to church, where mighty sport, to hear our clerke sing out of tune, though his master sits by him that begins and keeps the tune aloud for the parish." A speculation occurs to him as to the effect of music on a church offertory and possibly in producing a "cheerful giver." "Here was a collection for the sexton; but it came into my head why we should be more bold in making the collection while the psalm is singing, than in the sermon or prayer." A point to which Pepys gave some attention was that of learning "to trill," by which is meant, not a shake (on two notes), but what we should call vibrato (on one). He speaks

of going for a walk "humming to myself
(which nowadays is my constant practice
since I began to learn to sing) the trillo, and
find by use that it do come upon me."

The sound of Mr. Pepys "humming to
himself" roused his wife to emulation, and
in October 1661 he writes: "This morning
my wife and I lay long in bed, and amongst
other things fell into talk of musique, and
desired that I would let her learn to sing,
which I did consider, and promised her she
should. So before I rose, word was brought
me that my singing-master, Mr. Goodgroome, was come to teach me ; and so she
rose, and this morning began to learn also."
We have seen in an earlier chapter that
Mrs. Pepys's musical progress was not quite
unbroken, but many entries show us that
she advanced far enough to sing with her
husband and with their servants.

This brings us to a very noticeable point,
—the interest which Pepys took in the
musical powers of his servants. The first
member of the household who is mentioned
as musical is the "boy." "*Lord's Day,*

September 4.—The boy and I to singing of psalms, and then came in Mr. Hill, and he sung with us awhile; and he being gone, the boy and I again to the singing of Mr. Porter's [1] mottets, and it is a great joy to me that I am come to this condition to maintain a person in the house able to give me such pleasure as this boy do by his thorough knowledge of musique, as he sings any thing at first sight. Mr. Hill came to tell me that he had got a gentlewoman for my wife, one Mrs. Ferrabosco, that sings most admirably."

It is interesting to see Pepys thus early maintaining a musician in his house. We shall see later that after the conclusion of the Diary he went to considerable expense in supporting the Italian, Cesare Morelli, for the special purpose of being helped in his music. Morelli, too, as a Roman Catholic, was the unwitting cause of considerable trouble to Pepys, and led to his being for a time incarcerated in the Tower.

[1] Walter Porter was Master of the Choristers at Westminster Abbey.

LOVER OF MUSIQUE

Mrs. Ferrabosco was no doubt a connection of the well-known musicians of the same name. Of these, Alphonso Ferrabosco the younger was instructor in music to Prince Henry, to whom he dedicated a volume of "Ayres," published in 1609. This book contains a good many of the songs which were written for Ben Jonson's plays, set here with an accompaniment for the lute. Ben Jonson himself prefixed to the volume the following laudatory verses :—

To my excellent friend, Alphonso Ferrabosco.

"To urge, my loved Alfonso, that bold fame
  Of building towns and making wild beasts tame
  Which music had, or name her known effects,
  That she removeth cares, sadness ejects,
  Declineth anger, persuades clemency,
  Doth sweeten mirth, and heighten piety,
  And is to a body, often ill inclined,
  No less a sovereign cure than to the mind ;
  To allege that greatest men were not ashamed
  Of old, even by her practice, to be famed ;
  To say, indeed, she were the soul of heaven,
  That the eighth sphere, no less than Planets seven,
  Moved, by her order, and the ninth, more high,
  Including all, were thence called Harmony ;

69

I, yet, had utter'd nothing, on thy part,
When these were but the praises of the art.
But when I have said, The proofs of all these be
Shed in thy songs, 'tis true; but short of thee."

A few days later he sketches for us the
acquirements of the maid Mercer: "Back
again home, and there my wife and Mercer
and Tom and I sat till eleven at night, singing and fiddling, and a great joy it is to see
me master of so much pleasure in my house,
that it is and will be still, I hope, a constant
pleasure to me to be at home. The girle
plays pretty well upon the harpsicon, but
only ordinary tunes, but hath a good hand;
sings a little, but hath a good voyce and
eare. My boy, a brave boy, sings finely, and
is the most pleasant boy at present, while his
ignorant boy's tricks last, that ever I saw."
These "boy's tricks," however, were not
always an unmixed pleasure. Once he writes:
"I sent my boy home for some papers, where,
he staying longer than I would have him,
and being vexed at the business, and to be
kept from my fellows in the office longer
than was fit, I become angry, and boxed my

boy when he came, that I do hurt my thumb so much, that I was not able to stir all the day after, and in great pain." After a tiring day at the office, he could find refreshment in music. "Did the most at the office in that wearied and sleepy state I could, and so home to supper, and after supper falling to singing with Mercer did however sit up with her, she pleasing me with her singing of 'Helpe, helpe,' (one of his favourite Henry Lawes's songs) till past midnight, and I not a whit drowsy, and so to bed."

Mercer was a favourite pupil, and there is an account of Pepys taking down a song from the lips of Mrs. Knipp and afterwards teaching it to Mercer which must not be omitted.

"And here Knipp come to us, and I did take from her mouth the words and notes of her song of 'The Larke,' which pleases me mightily. Knipp tells us that there is a Spanish woman lately come over, that pretends to sing as well as Mrs. Knight; both of which I must endeavour to hear." A day or two later he writes: "So after a little supper, vexed, and spending a little time melancholy in making a base to the Larke's song, I to bed." The next day he gives Mercer a lesson in this song under the following original circumstances: "Thence to Unthanke's and 'Change, where wife did a little business while Mercer and I staid in the coach; and in a quarter of an hour, I taught her the whole Larke's song perfectly, so excellent an eare she hath."

The fact that a girl's manner of singing was attractive proved quite sufficient to outweigh many defects. "Home and there find my wife come home and hath brought her new girle I have helped her to, of Mr. Falconbridge's. She is wretched poor and but ordinary favoured; and we fain to lay out seven or eight pounds worth of clothes upon her back, which, methinks, do go against my heart; and I do not think I can ever esteem her as I could have done another that had come fine and handsome; and which is more, her voice, for want of use, is so furred, that it do not at present please me; but her manner of singing is such that

I shall, I think, take great pleasure in it. Well, she is come, and I wish us good fortune in her." Pepys paid great attention to the musical progress which his servants made, and in the account he has left us of a kind of examination he held in his family occurs some important information as to his own musical preferences. "*April* 12, 1667.—Then by water down to Redriffe, meaning to meet my wife, who is gone with Mercer, Barker and the boy (it being most sweet weather) to walk, and I did meet with them and walked back, and then by the time we got home it was dark, and we staid singing in the garden till supper was ready, and there was great pleasure. But I tried my girles Mercer and Barker singly one after another a single song, 'At dead low ebb,' &c., and I do clearly find that as to manner of singing the latter do much the better, the other thinking herselfe as I do myself above taking pains for a manner of singing, contenting ourselves with the judgment and goodness of eare." Pepys, in fact, aimed at singing with judgment—that is, intelligence and a just expression of the meaning in the words—and this principle, as here explicitly set forth, is quite consistent with his admiration for the songs of Henry Lawes, of which the distinguishing mark was the application of "just note and accent" to the words. The same enthusiasm is seen in the criticism he passes on the singing of one Mrs. Dutton. "After supper to talke and to sing, his man Dutton's wife singing very pleasantly (a mighty fat woman), and I wrote out one song from her and pricked the tune, both very pretty. But I did never heare one sing with so much pleasure to herself as this lady do, relishing it to her very heart, which was mighty pleasant." It is clear that those who sang with taste and enthusiasm, even if they had little knowledge of the art, had a sincere admirer in the amateur vocalist, Samuel Pepys.

CHAPTER V

PEPYS ON INSTRUMENTS, CHURCH MUSIC, &c.

THE constant references made by Pepys to various musical instruments show that his love for music was really genuine. Many an amateur begins and ends with vocal music. Pepys, we know, loved to sing, and spent much time in learning. But not only did he try to sing; he also practised on a considerable variety of instruments, and he mentions many more.

We know that he played upon the Treble Viol, the Lyra Viol, and the Bass Viol. This last seems also to have been played by Pepys's father, for he mentions sending his father's old Bass Viall to his brother Tom. But besides these he also mentions the Arched Viall, an instrument of which it seems no example exists. This Pepys

saw at a Musique Meeting at the Post
Office, "where I was once before," he adds,
"and thither anon come all the Gresham
College and a great deal of noble company,
and the new instrument was brought called
the Arched Viall, where being tuned with
lute strings and played on with kees like
an Organ, a piece of parchment is always
kept moving, and the strings which by the
kees are pressed down upon it are grated in
imitation of a bow by the parchment; and
so it is intended to resemble several vyalls
played on with one bow, but so basely and
harshly, that it will never do. But after
three hours' stay it could not be fixed in
tune, and so they were fain to go to some
other Musique of instruments which I am
grown quite out of love with."

Pepys here proved himself a discerning
critic. No doubt the world in general found
that the Arched Viall "would never do,"
and therefore no example has survived till
our own time.

In his early days the Lute seems to have
attracted most of his attention. We hear of

his accompanying Lady Wright's butler into the buttery, where the hospitable and artistic host gave him "sack and a lesson on his Lute, which he played very well." Pepys writes "*his* lute," for the good reason that his own instrument had been in pawn for some two years to Mr. Blagrave, one of the Gentlemen of the Chapel Royal. Some three months later he tells us that he called at Mr. Blagrave's, "when I took up my note that he had of me for 40s. which he two years ago did give me as a pawn while he had my lute—so that all things are now even between him and I." Pepys consulted Mr. Hill, the instrument maker, about alterations to both his lute and his vial. We know also that he played the Theorbo, a Bass Lute, for he refers to a visit from the above-mentioned Mr. Hill, who came to string it.

Possibly he played the Cittern also, for we find that at Dover on board ship after the landing of Charles II., Mr. Pepys, besides spending a great while in his cabin getting Lawes's song "Helpe, helpe!" without book, in response to the Admiral Lord Sandwich's invitation, and with the assistance of the lieutenant's Cittern and two candlesticks with money in them for cymbals, "made barber's music, with which my Lord was well-pleased." This mention of barber's music recalls the general custom of keeping a Cittern in a barber's shop, so that the person waiting to be shaved could pass the time pleasantly by playing until his turn came.

For the Guitar he had not much love, but was on a certain occasion given considerable trouble by the charge of one. This was the King's, and it was Pepys' duty to convey it from Dover to London. "I troubled much," he says, "with the King's gittar and Fair-brother the rogue, that I intrusted with the carrying of it on foot, whom I thought I had lost." Elsewhere he says he heard a French-man play "most extreme well" on it, but he adds, "methinks it is but a bauble." He tells us later that he spent an hour with Lord Sandwich, "my Lord playing upon the gittar, which he now commends above all musique in the world, because it is

base [1] enough for a single voice, and is so por-
table and manageable without much trouble."
Pepys in fact never came to respect the
guitar, for in 1667 he writes : "After done
with the Duke of York, and coming out
through his dressing-room I there spied
Signor Francisco tuning his gittar, and Monsieur de Puy with him, who did make him
play to me, which he did most admirably—
so well as I was mightily troubled that all
that pains should have been taken upon so
bad an instrument."

Another instrument akin to the Lute, the
Bandore or Pandore, is but once mentioned.
Pepys was staying at the Bear in Cambridge, and writes : "I could hardly sleep,
but waked very early, and when it was
time did call up Will and we rose, and
Musique (with a Bandore for the Base) did
give me a levett." This word levett is
derived from the French *lever*, a blast of
trumpets intended to awaken sleepers in the
morning.

[1] By "base" here he does not mean to disparage the
instrument, but that it is sufficient support to the voice.

The Dulcimer, again, Pepys did not play himself, but it did not escape his notice. He first saw it at a puppet play in Covent Garden. " Here among the fiddles I first saw a dulcimere played on with sticks knocking on the strings, and is very pretty." On another occasion he says : " In the next room one was playing very finely of the dulcimer, which well played I like well."

The least known among the instruments Pepys mentions, is the Trumpet-Marine. This is a stringed instrument having a triangular-shaped body or chest and a long neck, with a single string raised on a bridge and running along the body and neck. It was played with a bow. Hawkins in his " History of Music " refers very fully to the Trumpet-Marine, and quotes an extract from the *London Gazette* of February 4, 1674, giving an account of " a concert of four Trumpets-Marine never heard of before in England." The following entry by Pepys shows the above statement to be wrong : " To Charing Cross, there to see Polichinelli. But, it being begun, we in to see a

Frenchman, at the house, where my wife's father last lodged, one Monsieur Prin, play on the trump-marine, which he do beyond belief: and the truth is, it do so far out-do a trumpet as nothing more, and he do play anything very true, and it is most admirable and at first was a mystery to me that I should hear a whole concert of chords together at the end of a pause, but he showed me that it was only when the last notes were 5ths or 3rds, one to another, and then their sounds like an Echo did last so as they seemed to sound all together. The instrument is open at the end I discovered ; but he would not let me look into it, but I was mightily pleased with it, and he did take great pains to shew me all he could do on it, which was very much, and would make an excellent concert, two or three of them, better than trumpets can ever do, because of their want of compass."

The reason for this "Echo," which so astonished Mr. Pepys, was the presence of a large number of sympathetic strings inside the instrument. Had Pepys been allowed

to gratify his curiosity he would have seen
the cause of the effect which struck him.
The bridge of this instrument is movable
at one corner, and the vibration of this upon
the body of the instrument causes the extraordinary resemblance to an ordinary trumpet,
roughly and loudly played, to which no doubt
the name "trumpet-marine" is due. In
Molière's *Bourgeois Gentilhomme* M. Jourdain
shows his ignorance by wishing to add a
Trumpet-Marine to the instruments in his
concert: "Il y faudra mettre aussi une
trompette marine. La trompette marine
est un instrument qui me plaît, et qui est
harmonieux."

Act II. sc. I.

The last of the stringed instruments referred to by Pepys is the Virginal. It seems,
as Mr. Hipkins says, that during this period
all keyboard stringed instruments, in which
sound was produced by plucking the strings
with jacks, were known as Virginals. But
the word has also a narrower meaning,
namely, that of an oblong spinet, and it is
probably in this latter sense that Pepys
generally uses it. His allusions to it are

numerous and amusing. At the time of the Great Fire he tells us that the "River was full of lighters and boats taking in goods, and I observed that hardly one lighter or boat in three, that had the goods of a house in, but there was a pair of Virginals in it." And again: "They had a kinswoman, they call daughter, in the house, a short, ugly, red-haired slut, that plays upon the virginalls and sings, but after such a country manner I was weary of it, yet could not but commend it. So by and by after dinner comes Monsr. Gotier, who is beginning to teach her, but Lord! what a droll fellow it is to make her hold open her mouth, and telling her this and that so droll would make a man burst, but himself I perceive sings very well." This Gotier is no doubt the celebrated musician to whom Herrick alludes in his little poem in praise of Henry Lawes :—

> " Touch but thy lyre, my Harrie, and I hear
> From thee some raptures of the rare Gotere.
> Then if thy voice commingle with the string,
> I heare in thee rare Laniere to sing

Or curious Wilson : Tell me, canst thou be
Less than Apollo that usurp'st such three,
Three unto whom the whole world gives applause,
Yet their three praises praise but one; that's Lawes."

But on the whole Pepys distinctly preferred wind instruments to others. We
have seen how wind-music "wrapped up
his soul" when he heard it at the theatre,
so that he "remained all night transported,"
and throughout his Diary he never tires of
telling us how much he loved playing his
Flageolet. Not only did he play it himself,
but he had his wife taught this insinuating
instrument, and on all occasions when it
was possible he "took out his Flageolet
and piped." He uses it to fill up the
time "till a dish of poached eggs was got
ready for us," and when his day's work is
over he takes his Flageolet "and played
upon the leads in the garden where Sir W.
Pen came out in his shirt-sleeves onto his
leads, and then we staid talking and singing."
The master whom Pepys employed to teach
his wife was named Greeting, and we still
have copies of the Flagelet - Tutor which

this man published. Its title is "The Pleasant Companion or New Lessons and Instructions for the Flagelet, by Thomas Greeting, Gent." It contains an amusing preface, which exactly describes the companionship which Pepys found in his instrument. "The Flagelet is a very pleasant Instrument, and may be properly called Youth's Delight, by reason it may be carried in their Pocket with little or no trouble, walking in a Wood, or going by Water. It hath the advantage of other Instruments, being always in Tune, which other Instruments are not; and for those Youths and Young Ladies, whose Genius leads them to Musick, I know not a more easie and pleasant Instrument, than that we call the Flagelet: And though it may seem a little hard to Beginners, yet with the practice of a few hours, observing these Directions, and a little Assistance of a Master, the knowledge hereof may be readily attained unto."

In the copy of Greeting in the possession of the author there is to be found twice repeated a monogram consisting of the

HAIL TO THE MYRTILL SHADES

(From Greeting's "Flagelet Book." See Facsimile opposite.)

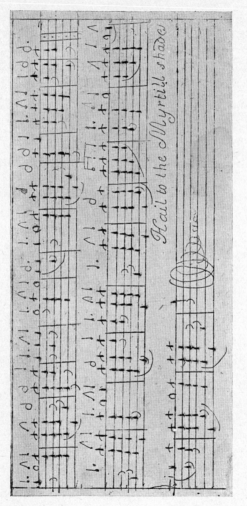

Hail to the Myrtill shade

To face p. 86

letters S. P. Dr. Edward Scott, of the British Museum, thinks there can be little doubt that the monogram is written by Pepys, and if that is so, no doubt this copy originally belonged to Pepys himself.

Pepys also mentions another well-known variety of this instrument, the Double Flageolet. "To Dumbleby's, the pipe-maker, there to advise about the making of a flageolet to go low and soft, and he do show me a way which do do, and also a fashion of having two pipes of the same note fastened together so as I can play on one and then echo it upon the other, which is mighty pretty."

The Recorder or Beaked Flute is not mentioned until late in the Diary, 1668, and affords evidence of the continued and increasing interest which Pepys took in music. "To Dumbleby's and there did talk a great deal about pipes; and did buy a recorder, which I do intend to learn to play on, the sound of it being of all sounds in the world most pleasing to me." This instrument is referred to in the famous scene in *Hamlet*—III. II. line 286.

Ham. Come, some music! come, the recorders!—

For if the king like not the comedy,

Why, then, belike,—he likes it not, perdy.—

Come, some music!

Then comes the scene with the two friends, and at the end of it we have the stage-direction "re-enter players with recorders," and Hamlet continues— *lin 336*

Ham. O, the recorders!—let me see one.—To withdraw with you :—why do you go about to recover the wind of me, as if you would drive me into a toil?

Guil. O, my lord, if my duty be too bold, my love is too unmannerly.

Ham. I do not well understand that. Will you play upon this pipe?

Guil. My lord, I cannot.

Ham. I pray you.

Guil. Believe me, I cannot.

Ham. I do beseech you.

Guil. I know no touch of it, my lord.

Ham. It is as easy as lying : govern these ventages with your fingers and thumb, give it breath with your mouth, and it will discourse most eloquent music. Look you, these are the stops.

Guil. But these cannot I command to any utterance of harmony ; I have not the skill.

Ham. Why, look you now, how unworthy a thing you make of me! You would play upon me; you would seem to know my stops; you would sound me from my lowest note to the top of my compass; and there is much music, excellent voice, in this little organ; yet cannot you make it speak. 'Sblood, do you think I am easier to be played on than a pipe? Call me what instrument you will, though you can fret me, yet you cannot play upon me.

This instrument seems to have made Pepys take to studying music with some extra attention. "So home to my chamber," he writes, "to be fingering of my Recorder, and getting of the Scale of Musique without book, which I at last see is necessary for a man that would understand musique as it is now taught to understand, though it be a ridiculous and troublesome way, and I know I shall be able hereafter to show the world a simpler way; but like the old hypotheses in philosophy, it must be learned though a man knows a better." This entry is obscure. Pepys can hardly mean that he was learning the scale for the first time; probably he refers to the special fingering of the Recorder.

The very next night he enters in his journal:
" Home, and then to the perfecting my
getting the scale of musique without book,
which I have done to perfection backward
and forward ; " and on the following night
he merely puts " Conning my gamut."

All this love for instrumental music was
not shared by one of Pepys' friends, Lord
Lauderdale. The diarist went to Lord
Lauderdale's house (situated, it is said, on
Highgate Hill, and now known as Waterlow
Park), and he tells us he found " him and
his lady and some Scotch people at supper.
Pretty odd company, though my Lord
Brouncker tells me my Lord Lauderdale
is a man of mighty good reason and jugement. But at supper there played one of
their servants upon the viallin some Scotch
tunes only, several and the best of their
country as they seemed to esteem them, by
their praising and admiring them ; but—
Lord, the strangest ayre that ever I heard in
my life, and all of one cast. But strange to
hear my Lord Lauderdale say himself that
he had rather hear a cat mew than the best

musique in the world; and the better the
musique, the more sicke it makes him, and
that of all instruments he hates the lute
most, and next to that, the bagpipe."

Lastly, Pepys gives us various references
to organs. For instance, he goes "to
Hackney . . . and here I was told that at
their church they have a fair pair of organs,
which play while the people sing, which I
am mightily glad of, wishing the like at our
church at London, and would give £50
towards it." He would always go out of
his way to see an organ, as, indeed, he would
to see most things; and he writes: "Thence
to the Exchange; while meeting Dr. Gibbons
there, he and I to see an organ at the Dean
of Westminster's lodgings at the Abby,
the Bishop of Rochester's." Similarly on his
visit to The Hague he notices that there were
very fine organs in the churches, and he
jots down in his Diary that on a certain
June 17 (Lord's Day) "the Organs did
begin to play at Whitehall before the
king." In April 1661 he went to Rochester
and "there saw the Cathedrall, which is

now fitting for use, and the organ then a-tuning."

From organs it is but a short step to the choirs which they accompanied. Here, too, his opinion is expressed with perfect frankness, but he is not without the ordinary human prejudice in favour of a comfortable seat. On February 28, 1664, he writes: "Up and walked to Paul's. But before and after sermon I was impatiently troubled at the Quire—the worst that ever I heard." As regards the Abbey, he tells us that he there heard the church service read "very ridiculously." This may, however, refer to the clergy rather than the choir, for a few months later Pepys "met Mr. Hooper, and he took me in among the quire, and there I sang with them their service." But his warmest commendation is reserved for St. George's, Windsor: "So took coach and to Windsor, to the Garter, and thither sent for Dr. Childe; who come to us, and carried us to St. George's Chappell; and there placed us among the Knights' stalls (and pretty the observation, that no man, but a woman, may sit in a Knight's place, where any brass-plates are set); and hither come cushions to us, and a young singing-boy to bring us a copy of the anthem to be sung. And here, for our sakes, had this anthem and the great service sung extraordinary, only to entertain us. It is a noble place indeed, and a good Quire of voices." Such is the soothing effect of a knight's stall and a copy of the music.

Of this Dr. Child, the following anecdote is told, for the true version of which we are indebted to the researches of Mr. Barclay Squire, set forth in the "Dictionary of National Biography." It appears that after the Civil War about £500 was owing to Child as arrears of salary. One day, despairing of ever receiving so large a sum from the King, he declared in the presence of some of the Canons of Windsor that he would gladly give up his right to the £500 for £5 down and some bottles of wine. The Canons took him at his word, and a formal agreement on the subject was drawn up and signed. When, however, James II. succeeded to the throne, one of his first actions was to pay off arrears which had been left unpaid by his brother. Then, as our authority put it, Child "repined," but was generously released by the Canons from his agreement, on condition that he paved the body of the choir at St. George's, Windsor, with marble. This he did, and the fact is recorded on his tomb.

CHAPTER VI

PEPYS AS THEORIST AND COMPOSER

THE Theory of Music was a subject which had great fascination for Pepys, and an interesting proof of this is the mention he makes at various times of the most noted works on the subject. He mentions early Morley's celebrated "Plaine and Easie Introduction to Musique." "Having a cold so as I am not able to speak, I lay in bed till noon, and then up and to my chamber with a good fire, and there spent an hour on Morley's Introduction to Musique, a very good but unmethodical book." Again, he mentions another celebrated treatise. "Walked to Woolwich all the way reading Playford's Introduction to Musick, wherein are some things very pretty." Later on we find him thinking for himself on the subject. He begins to be dissatisfied with the ideas set forth. He spends a morning "trying some conclusions upon my viall in order to the inventing a better Theory of Musick than hath yet been abroad," and he adds: "I think verily I shall do it." At this time he is plainly dissatisfied with our English music, for he goes to the Queen's Chapel, "and there did hear the Italians sing; and, indeed, their musique did appear most admirable to me, beyond anything of ours; I was never so well satisfied in my life with it." He is still convinced that he *can* do something towards inventing a better theory. He goes "to Bishopsgate St. thinking to have found a Harpsicon-maker that used to live there before the fire, but he is gone, and I have a mind forthwith to have a little Harpsicon made me to confirm and help me in my musique notions, which my head is nowadays full of, and I do believe will come to something that is very good." A week later he has Mr. Banister (whom Pepys calls "the great Master of Musique"), and has "very good discourse with him about musique, so confirming some of my new

notions about musique that it puts me upon
a resolution to go on and make a scheme
and theory of musique—not yet ever made in
the world."

One does not know what direction his
thoughts took, but it is interesting to note
that a few days later he was actually dis-
cussing Acoustics. The entry is so important
that no apology is necessary for inserting it
in full. "Thence with Lord Brouncker to
the Royall Society, where they were just
done; but there I was forced to subscribe
to the building of a College, and did give
£40; and several others did subscribe, some
greater and some less sums, but several I
saw hang off; and I doubt it will spoil the
Society, for it breeds faction and ill-will, and
becomes burdensome to some that cannot,
or would not, do it. Here to my great con-
tent I did try the use of the Otacousticon,
which was only a great glass bottle broke at
the bottom, putting the neck to my eare,
and there I did plainly hear the dashing of
the oares of the boats in the Thames to
Arundell gallery window, which, without it,

I could not in the least do, and may I believe be improved to a great height, which I am mighty glad of. Thence with Lord Brouncker and several of them to the King's Head Taverne by Chancery Lane, and there did eat and drink, and talk, and, above the rest, I did hear of Mr. Hooke and my Lord an account of the reason of concords and discords in musique, which they say is from the equality of vibrations; but I am not satisfied in it, but will at my leisure think of it more, and see how far that do go to explain it."

Now that he is seriously studying theory, we find him seeking a celebrated French treatise by Mersenne, "a man that has wrote well of musique, but it is not to be had, but I have given order for its being sent for over; and I did here buy Des Cartes his little treatise of Musique." The latter work he tells us later "he understood not, nor think he did well that wrote it, though a most learned man." But with Mersenne it was a different story: "In the office being pleased that this morning my bookseller brings me home Marcennus's book of musick, which costs me £3, 2s., but is a very fine book."

Pepys began composition in February 1662. " At night begun to compose songs, and begun with ' Gaze not on Swans,' " and a little later we read : " Long with Mr. Birkenshaw in the morning at my musique practice, finishing my song of ' Gaze not on Swans' in two parts, which pleases me well, and I did give him £5 for this month or five weeks that he hath taught me, which is a great deal of money and troubled me to part with it." This song does not now exist, though there is one to the same words by Henry Lawes.

The earliest song still remaining to us is his setting of " Beauty Retire," the words of Solyman to Roxolana in the " Siege of Rhodes." *by Sir William Davenant*

Of the song " Beauty Retire " there are two settings in the Pepysian library. They are not altogether unlike each other, the key being the same, and the rhythm very similar. But one (printed in Mr. Wheatley's edition, and assigned by him to Pepys) occurs in a collection of things by an Italian, one Morelli. This collection is described by Pepys as being a collection of " Songs and other Compositions, Light, Grave, and Sacred, for a single voice, adjusted to the particular compass of mine, with a Th. Bass on ye Guitar by Cesare Morelli." It is possible that this was an amplification of the original setting, made by Morelli, who lived with Pepys and assisted him in his music some years after the period of the Diary, as he states later.

But whether this version be Morelli's or not, it is certain that to the other we must look for Pepys's composition. The proof of this lies in the fact that the portrait of Pepys by Hayles in the National Portrait Gallery shows the first few bars of " Beauty Retire." He is holding the composition in his hand, and the music can be plainly read. Now this setting is not the one we have ascribed to Morelli, but the other. It is true that in the picture the key is different. This may, however, be the original key and would be suitable to a woman's voice, for instance Knipp's, while the setting in the MS. would be as Mr. Pepys himself sang it. There can be little doubt that Pepys's version came first, and that the other is much later, for as we shall see presently, Morelli belongs altogether to the later part of the diarist's musical life, and is never even mentioned in the Diary itself.

The song is first mentioned on December 6, 1665 : "I spent the afternoon upon a song of Solyman's words to Roxolana that I have set." This is followed on December 11 by the intelligence : "To Mr. Hill, and sang among other things my song of 'Beauty Retire,' which he likes, only excepts against two notes in the base, but likes the whole very well." The next mention is on February 23, 1666, as follows : "Comes Mrs. Knipp to see my wife, and I spent all the evening talking with this baggage, and teaching her my song of 'Beauty Retire,' which she sings and makes go most rarely—and a very fine song it seems to be." And again elsewhere : "After our first bout of dancing,

Knipp and I to sing, and Mercer and Captain Downing, who loves and understands Musick, would by all means have my song of 'Beauty Retire,' which Knipp had spread abroad, and he extols it above anything he ever heard." His teaching of Knipp seems to have had its reward, for in yet another place he writes: "Here we had ale and cakes, and mighty merry, and sung my song, which she (Knipp) now sings bravely, and makes me proud of myself."

The next song on which Pepys embarked, and the only one besides "Beauty Retire" which we possess, was "It is Decreed." This was begun on April 5, 1666. The words are also by Ben Jonson, and the subject seems to have appealed to Pepys, for three weeks later he tells us: "In all my ridings in the coach and intervals my mind hath been full these three weeks of setting to musique 'It is decreed.'" It was a hard task, and three months later we read: "I home, and then after a little while making of my tune to 'It is decreed'—to bed." About a month later: "Mrs. Knipp tells me my song of

'Beauty Retire' is mightily cried up, which I am not a little proud of, and do think I have done 'It is decreed' better, *but I have not finished it*." Later still, in November, he says : "After church home and I to my chamber, and there did finish the putting time to my song of 'It is decreed,' and do please myself *at last*, and think it will be thought a good song."

It was not long, in fact only three days, before the composer began to teach his favourite Mrs. Knipp what he calls his "new Recitativo of 'It is decreed,' of which," he adds, "she learnt a good part, and I do well like it, and believe shall be well pleased when she hath it all, and that it will be found an agreeable thing." It is to the credit of the composer that he took such pains, and spoke on the whole so modestly of his effort. No doubt he had merely fitted a melody to the rather bombastic words, and had put no accompaniment, for about a month later he writes : "Then I to begin setting a base to 'It is decreed.'" His "base" was not satisfactory, for a week later he met "Mr. Hingston, the organist (my old acquaintance), and I took him to the Dog Taverne, and got him to set me a Base to my 'It is decreed,' which I think will go well, but he commends the song not knowing the words, but says the ayre is good, and believes the words are plainly expressed. He is of my mind against having 8ths unnecessarily in composition. This did all please me mightily." The artful Mr. Hingston evidently found consecutive octaves between the bass that Mr. Pepys had begun to set and the melody of the song, and broke it gently to the composer.

At this same interview Mr. Hingston gave the diarist a pitiful account of the state of affairs in the King's Band. "Many of the Musique are ready to starve, they being five years behindhand for their wages; nay, Evens the famous man upon the Harp, having not his equal in the world, did the other day die for mere want, and was fain to be buried of the alms of the parish, and carried to his grave in the dark at night without one linke, but that Mr. Hingston met it by chance and

did give 12d. to buy two or three links. He
says all must come to ruin at this rate, and
I believe him." Hingston was a pupil of
Orlando Gibbons, and served under Charles I.,
Cromwell, and Charles II.

Mr. Hingston's Base was a success, for on
Christmas Day, 1666, Pepys "having dined
well on some good ribs of beef roasted and
mince pies" (which Mrs. Pepys, poor wretch,
had sat up till four in the morning seeing
her maids make), "and having my wife, my
brother, and Barker to dinner, and plenty of
good wine of my own, and my heart full of
true joy—after dinner I began to teach my
wife and Barker my song, 'It is decreed,'
which pleases me mightily, as now I have
Mr. Hingston's Base." Mercer had a lesson
in the song a week or two later, and Barker
also, "which," he says, "she will sing
prettily." It is likely they found the song
difficult, for no references to it appear for a
whole year, when again Mercer is being
taught "It is decreed." Probably the ladies
never did master the song, for three months
later Mr. Pepys began to "prick out 'It is

decreed,' intending to have it ready to give Mr. Harris on Thursday for him to sing, believing that he will do it more right than a woman that sings better, unless it were Knipp, which I cannot have opportunity to teach it to."

Though we naturally know most of Pepys's musical life during the period of the Diary, yet it must not be supposed that his enthusiasm abated in later years. He became, of course, a more prominent public servant, and his time was therefore more occupied, but the old fire is there still, and in 1674 he can still write of " musique, in which my utmost luxury still lies." One great proof that he kept up his musical studies lies in the fact that he took into his house the Italian, Cesare Morelli, in order to have some one to help him whenever he could spare time for music. This Morelli is an important figure in Pepys's life after the Diary closes, and a short sketch of his career will be of interest.

Born in Flanders and bred at Rome, he was, at the time when he was first recommended to Pepys, in the service of a nobleman at Lisbon. He was sent to Pepys by his friend Mr. Hill, and was described as having a most admirable voice, and singing rarely to his theorbo and with great skill. "His manner of singing," says Hill, "is alla Italiana di tutta perfettione." Pepys, in a very frank and characteristic letter, describes to Hill, and through him to us, the way in which he takes his gradual rise in the world. "Nothing," he says, "which has yet or may further happen towards the rendering me more conspicuous in the world, has led or can ever lead to the admitting any alteration in the little methods of my private way of living; as having not in my nature any more aversion to sordidness than I have to pomp, and in particular to that sort of it which consists in the length of such a train (I mean of servants for state only) as the different humour of some and greater quality of others do sometimes call for." But if the young Morelli can put up with his "silent and unencumbered guise of life," he is willing to take him into his service, and to pay him £30 a year, with his lodging and entertainment.

So Morelli became a member of Pepys's household, and no doubt rendered his employer great assistance in his musical studies. But a storm was coming which made it necessary for the two to part company. At the beginning of 1679 (four years after Morelli's arrival in England) Pepys was accused of being a Roman Catholic, and of plotting to dethrone the King. In support of this it was alleged that Morelli, who lived in his house, was no musician but a disguised Jesuit. Pepys's enemies managed to secure his committal to the Tower in May 1679, though he was eventually released on bail. In the end the charge was not proceeded with, but Pepys had at the end of 1678 requested Morelli to move from his house to Brentwood, having first vainly tried to induce him to abjure his religion and turn Protestant. In a letter still extant Morelli writes to assure Pepys that many could bear witness to his not having been known at Lisbon as a priest, much less as a Jesuit.

" Had I been such," he says, " I should have been obliged, on pain of excommunication, to clothe myself as a priest in Portugal, instead of living at Lisbon four years in the same dress I wear here."

But though Morelli was no longer in his house, Pepys did not cease to correspond with him and consult him on musical matters. In September 1679 he writes to him that he wished Morelli were present, for then " I would have consulted with you about the use of the table which you have given me for the guitar ; for the little knowledge in musique which I have, never was of more use to me than it is now, under the molestations of mind which I have at this time, more than ordinary, to contend with. Therefore I would be glad to improve that little knowledge as far as I could, to making myself capable, by the help of your table, of playing a basse-continuë, which I would not despair of doing in a tolerable degree, after you shall have made me master of that table." Therefore he proposes to visit Morelli for a day, " having nothing remaining in my hands to practise upon but the Lamentations of Jeremiah."

Even more than a year later Pepys, though keeping up his intimacy with Morelli, is still afraid of the charge of Popery. He asks Morelli, when he comes up to London, to see that his "stay be no longer than is just necessary." The same enemies apparently were ready to take any opportunity of injuring him. "But," he adds, "I hope God Almighty will, in His due time, deliver us from the 'lying tongues' mentioned in your last anthem—for which this gives me occasion of again thanking you, as being words very well chosen with respect to my present case, and those words well set." In April of the same year Morelli wrote to Pepys to sympathise with him in an illness, and also to give his opinion of some music Pepys had sent him for criticism. The letter is worth quoting in full.

11th April 1681.

HONOURED SIR,—I did receive your last letter with much grief having an account of your painful feaver. I Pray God it will not vex your body too much, and if by chance it should vex you longer, there is here a man that can cure it with simpathetical powder, if you please to send me down the pearinghs of the nailes of both your hands and your foots, and three locks of hair of the top of your crown.   I hope with the grace of God it will cure you.

As for the compositions of them two masters, on my jugement (though weak) I like better Baptist's works than Pedro's, because Baptist work masterly as you will perceive betwixt their bases. All Baptist's bases are singable where many of Pedro's are not so.—Herewith my humble respects, remains, honoured sir, your most grateful servant,   CESARE MORELLI.

Baptist is no doubt the Italian musician See Page 55 who is mentioned by Pepys in 1667 as having at Lord Brouncker's house sung through an act of an opera which he had just composed.   Pepys admired it greatly. Who Pedro was is more doubtful.   Possibly he was the Italian whom Pepys had at his house on one occasion with other singers. He calls him "a slovenly and ugly fellow, who sings Italian songs to the Theorbo most See Page 59. neatly."

Morelli must after this have returned to

111

the Continent. We possess, however, one more letter of his written from Brussels more than five years later, on November 23, 1686. He has heard that the King, James II., is about to form a choir for his chapel, and he writes to ask Pepys to get him a place in it. Whether he was successful or not does not appear. That Morelli taught others than Pepys appears from an incidental mention of him in Roger North's Autobiography. Speaking of a young lady to whom he was somewhat attracted, North tells us that " she mastered that puzzling instrument the Lute, and having a good voice and the instruction of an Italian—one Signor Morelli—she acquired to sing exceeding well after the Italian manner, to her own playing upon the Lute or Guitar." From this point Morelli vanishes from Pepys's life, but the intimate terms on which the two stood show that Pepys kept alive his musical interests even when the pressure of public business became more severe.

This appears also very clearly in the Diary which he kept of his expedition to Tangier.

It shows the estimation in which Pepys was held, that when Charles II. sent out ships and men to demolish the works at Tangier, and to bring home the garrison, Pepys was sent to decide the various questions as to compensation for property destroyed, and the like, which were sure to arise. He himself describes for us the errand on which he was sent : " My own part is adjudging the civil proprieties between the King and the burghers. In that, I trust in God, I shall leave as little dissatisfaction on the proprietors' part (governing myself by doing as I would be done by) as it is expected I should prevent any impostures on his Majesty." Pepys himself approved of Charles's policy towards Tangier, and evidently disliked the town on other grounds, for in the same letter to his friend Houblon, from which we have just quoted, he writes with an honest, affectionate touch that reminds us of the Diary : "I would not wish my sweet W. or little Jemmy here ; for with sorrow and indignation I speak ; it is a place of the world I would last send a young man to,

H

but to hell. Therefore, on God's account as well as the King's, I think it high time it were dissolved."

If Pepys had been the old roué that he is too often called, he would not have felt this "sorrow and indignation." Those who emphasise the less respectable features of the Diary forget that it lays bare the intimate daily life of a *young* man. Pepys was in his twenty-seventh year when he began to write, and he gave up the Diary when but just entering his thirty-eighth. Indeed the touching words with which he lays down his pen, memorable enough for their own sake, are sufficient answer to those who ignorantly denounce the writer as an *old* rascal or a vain *old* man. "And thus ends all that I doubt I shall ever be able to do with my own eyes in the keeping of my Journal, I being not able to do it any longer, having done now so long as to undo my eyes almost every time that I take a pen in my hand; and therefore whatever comes of it I must forbear; and therefore resolve, from this time forward, to have it kept by my people in longhand, and must be contented to set down no more than is fit for them and all the world to know; or if there be anything, which cannot be much, *now my amours are past*, and my eyes hindering me in almost all other pleasures, I must endeavour to keep a margin in my book open, to add here and there a note in short-hand in my own hand. And so I betake myself to that course, which is almost as much as to see myself go in to my grave : for which, and all the discomforts that will accompany my being blind, the good God prepare me!" With this outburst of genuine feeling ringing in our ears, we can hardly doubt that Pepys had once and for all put aside the follies of his youth. Indeed the records of his after life abound in evidences of the good work done for his King and country, for science, and for art.

That he did his work well at Tangier we can gather from the letter Lord Dartmouth, the head of the expedition, writes to him on their return. In it he says : "Though I can never sufficiently acknowledge all your favours in this service, yet my true thank-fulness and gratitude to you shall never be wanting. I hope you found his Majesty satisfied in your service, otherwise I can never hope he will be in mine."

This Tangier Diary or Journal has not the fulness or the self-revelation of the earlier one, but it contains sufficient charac-teristic touches to make it very interesting reading. From it we see that Pepys was able to gratify his taste for music on the voyage. Indeed, he writes to his friend Evelyn from Portsmouth while he was quite ignorant of the object for which he was being sent to Tangier, and includes music among the attractions which he promises himself. " What our work, nevertheless, is, I am not solicitous to learn, nor forward to make griefs at, it being handled by our masters as a secret. This only I am sure of, that over and above the satisfaction of being thought fit for some use or other ('tis no matter what), I shall go in a good ship, with a good fleet, under a very worthy leader, in a conversation as delightful as companions in the first form in divinity, law, physic, and the usefullest parts of mathematics can render it, namely, Dr. Ken, Dr. Trumbull, Dr. Lawrence, and Mr. Sheres ; with the additional pleasure of concerts (much above the ordinary) of voices, flutes, and violins ; and to fill up all (if anything can do it where Mr. Evelyn is wanting), good humour, good cheer, some good books, the company of my nearest friend, Mr. Hewer, and a reasonable prospect of being home again in less than two months." Of this company Evelyn writes that "they seem to carry along with them not a colony only, but a college, nay, an whole university ; all the sciences, all the arts, and all the professors of them too."

One of the company, however, was to return ingloriously before the rest. When they reached Tangier, Dr. Trumbull was, as Pepys says, "so weak and sheepish," and exhibited such a "ridiculous melancholy," that at last Lord Dartmouth, observing that Pepys did all the work, and that Trumbull signified little, resolved to send the latter home. Of this departure, and the feelings with which the rest of them viewed it, we have an amusing description quite in Pepys' early and most graphic style. "*Oct.* 20, 1683. *Saturday.*— Ending letter; Dr. Trumbull still ridiculously impatient to be gone. But it was afternoon before my Lord had done. Then, all of us took our leaves, with all the respect in the world, that he might be useful in England" (*i.e.* useful to Pepys and his friends). "My Lord came with him to my chamber, and the governor, Kirke, being with us, we drank a parting bottle to his good voyage. We all walked down, saw him in the boat, and gave him several guns from the town. *So the fool went away, every creature of the house laughing at him.*" Here we recognise the old shrewdness of the diarist.

That the art of music at any rate was represented on the voyage is borne out by the various entries during that period. While still in touch of Portsmouth, Pepys dines on board the *Royal Mary*, and records "many songs among the gentlemen and

commanders." On one occasion he sits up
" till midnight, on the quarter-deck, seeing
the seamen dance to the harp and song," on
another, " after dinner, in the cabin, musick
and good humour." He dines with Sir J.
Berry in the *Henrietta*, and after dinner
" he and a reformado captain played on the
violin," and when they are off Cadiz he
puts down " Night, mighty pretty music on
the flute."

But as soon as Tangier was reached Pepys
had too much work to spare time for music,
and there are but few references to it. Except for one entry of a visit " to Captain
St. John's; a good supper, and a harp well
played on," such distractions as he had were
of a different kind. He has " the pleasure
of again seeing fine Mrs. Kirke, better
dressed than before, but yet short of what
I have known her," or he entertains himself
in Hakluyt's " English Voyages, Navigations,
Traffics, and Discoveries," to his mighty
pleasure.

Towards the end of his life we hear little
of his musical tastes. He was, however,

pestered by those who wished him to hear vocalists sing. A Lady Tuke wrote in 1686 asking him to hear one Signor Cefache, and adds, "he also designs to bring Batiste with him to play on the harpsichord, I having told him you have the best in England, and are a great lover of music." We have also a letter written by his nephew, Jackson, as late as 1699, which shows that Pepys in his retirement at Clapham, still had the same enthusiasm as of old, and still liked to hear who were helping forward the art which he loved. Speaking of his stay in Rome, Jackson tells his uncle among other things of "Paluccio, an admired young performer, singing, and Corelli, the famous Violin, playing in concert with above 30 more."

So we may take leave of Mr. Pepys, his viols, his songs, and his friends. Nor can we sum up better the impression—"votiva veluti descripta tabella"—which his unique history of himself leaves on our minds, than by quoting the words with which his friend and fellow-diarist, Evelyn, records his death. —"1703. *May* 26. This day died Mr.

Samuel Pepys, a very worthy, industrious, and curious person, none in England exceeding him in knowledge of the navy, in which he had passed through all the most considerable offices, Clerk of the Acts and Secretary of the Admiralty, all which he performed with great integrity. When King James II. went out of England he laid down his office, and would serve no more ; but withdrawing himself from all public affairs, he lived at Clapham with his partner, Mr. Hewer, formerly his clerk, in a very noble house and sweet place, where he enjoyed the fruit of his labours in great prosperity. He was universally beloved, hospitable, generous, learned in many things, skilled in music, a very great cherisher of learned men of whom he had the conversation."

BEAUTY RETIRE

The Accompaniment Arranged by SIR FREDERICK BRIDGE.[1]

Composed by SAMUEL PEPYS.

Beau-ty Re-tire, thou doest my pit-ty move, Be-lieve my pit-ty, and then trust my love. Att first I thought her by our Pro-phet sent

As a re-ward for Va-lour's toiles, More worth than all my Fa-ther's spoils, But now shee is be-come my pun-ish-ment; But

Thou art just, O Pow'r Di-vine, With new and pain-ful arts of stu-died war I breake the hearts of halfe the world, and Shee breakes mine!

[1] The melody and bass are exactly as they stand in the Pepys MS. The harmony is filled in from the original figured bass—the arranger is responsible for the marks of expression.

To face p. 123.

INDEX

123

INDEX

INDEX

Laniere, W., 57

Lauderdale, Lord, hates music, 91

Lawes, Henry, 18; "The Royal Slave," 18; connected with "Comus," 19; composes "Tavola," 21; Orpheus' hymn, 24; "Helpe, helpe," 71; death, 23

Lawes, William, 25; siege of Chester, 25

Levett, a, 79

Lock, Matthew, meets Pepys, 14; his Kyrie, 17

Lully, 27

Marshall, Becke, 7

Master of the Music, the, 45

Mercer taught to sing, 1

Mersenne's treatise, Pepys' opinion of, 98

Milton and Lawes, 19, 20

Morelli, 106 *seq.*; letter to Pepys proposing a cure, 110; and James II.'s choir, 112

Morley's "Introduction to Musique," Pepys' opinion, 95

North, Mr., plays well at first sight, 10

North, Roger, quoted, 15, 47; and Morelli, 112

Organ, at Whitehall, 29; at Hackney, at Dean of West- minster's lodgings, at The Hague, at Rochester Cathe- dral, 91

Otacousticon, the, 97

Parry, Sir Hubert, quoted, 20

Pedro, Seignor, 59

Pepys, Samuel, fears to give too much time to music, 11; criticises elaborate vocal music, 50; never lived so merrily as in plague-time, 58; on weekly music-meet- ings, 60; sings in Chapel Royal, 62; forced to com- mend bad singing, 65; on church-offertories, 66; learns to trill, 66; examines his servants in music, 73; thinks he can invent a better theory of music, 96; at Royal Society, subscribes towards building a college, 97; dis- cusses acoustics, 97; ob- jects to consecutive octaves in composition, 104; com- mitted to the Tower, 108; character defended, 114

Pepys, Mrs., taught to sing, 6; learns the flageolet, 8

Petition of King's Band *re* Banister, 42; answer to ditto, 46

Playford's "Introduction to Musique," Pepys' opinion, 95

Porter's mottets, 68

125

INDEX

Printed by BALLANTYNE, HANSON & Co.
Edinburgh & London.